The Dark Side of
PETER PAN

The Dark Side of
PETER PAN

J.M. BARRIE, THE MAN WHO COULDN'T GROW UP

OLIVIA CAMOZZI

WHITE OWL
AN IMPRINT OF PEN & SWORD BOOKS LTD.
YORKSHIRE – PHILADELPHIA

First published in Great Britain in 2024 by
PEN AND SWORD WHITE OWL
An imprint of
Pen & Sword Books Ltd
Yorkshire - Philadelphia

Copyright © Olivia Camozzi, 2024

ISBN 978 1 39904 755 5

The right of Olivia Camozzi to be identified as Author of this work has been asserted by her in accordance with the Copyright, Designs and Patents Act 1988.

A CIP catalogue record for this book is available from the British Library.

All rights reserved. No part of this book may be reproduced or transmitted in any form or by any means, electronic or mechanical including photocopying, recording or by any information storage and retrieval system, without permission from the Publisher in writing.

Typeset in Times New Roman 11/14.5 by
SJmagic DESIGN SERVICES, India.
Printed and bound in the UK by CPI Group (UK) Ltd.

Pen & Sword Books Ltd incorporates the Imprints of Pen & Sword Books Archaeology, Atlas, Aviation, Battleground, Discovery, Family History, History, Maritime, Military, Naval, Politics, Railways, Select, Transport, True Crime, Fiction, Frontline Books, Leo Cooper, Praetorian Press, Seaforth Publishing, Wharncliffe and White Owl.

For a complete list of Pen & Sword titles please contact
PEN & SWORD BOOKS LIMITED
George House, Units 12 & 13, Beevor Street, Off Pontefract Road,
Barnsley, South Yorkshire, S71 1HN, England
E-mail: enquiries@pen-and-sword.co.uk
Website: www.pen-and-sword.co.uk

or
PEN AND SWORD BOOKS
1950 Lawrence Rd, Havertown, PA 19083, USA
E-mail: uspen-and-sword@casematepublishers.com
Website: www.penandswordbooks.com

Contents

Acknowledgements vii

Prologue ix

Chapter 1   All children, except one, grow up 1

Chapter 2   I don't want ever to be a man 10

Chapter 3   There is something she wants to be to me, but she says it is not my mother 14

Chapter 4   There never was a simpler happier family until the coming of Peter Pan 25

Chapter 5   Come away, come away! 35

Chapter 6   "Do you know," Peter asked, "why swallows build in the eaves of houses? It is to listen to the stories" 47

Chapter 7   So the older ones have become glassy-eyed and seldom speak... but the little ones still wonder 56

Chapter 8   "If only you could be this way forever!" 67

Chapter 9   Never is an awfully long time 83

Chapter 10 They are the eyes a mother leaves behind to guard her children 94

Chapter 11 Stars are beautiful, but they may not take part in anything, they must just look on forever 105

Chapter 12 Peter was not quite like other boys; but he was afraid at last 114

Chapter 13 Do you believe in fairies? 121

Chapter 14   You can have anything in life if you will sacrifice everything else for it.. 130

Chapter 15   The moment you doubt whether you can fly, you cease for ever to be able to do it.................................. 136

Chapter 16   To die will be an awfully big adventure 146

Chapter 17   I suppose it's like the ticking crocodile, isn't it? Time is chasing after all of us 154

Epilogue 162

Sources 173

Notes 176

Acknowledgements

Writing this biography was a surprise project for me since I never saw myself writing anything non-fiction, but after being exposed to the idea I ran away with it and found myself deep in research, planning and working towards a deadline. None of this would've been possible without a string of people that led to the publication of this book.

First and foremost, I have to thank Matthew Lewis for introducing me to Pen and Sword Books, who have proved themselves to be the best group of people to be working together in a publishing house. Although Matthew's expertise lies in a completely different time period, and he insists he did nothing, the ball would never have started rolling without him and his kindness towards someone he barely knew.

To my commissioning editor, Jonathan Wright – it's incredibly difficult to break into this industry, and all a young writer needs is for someone to take a chance on them. Jonathan took that chance on me.

I would like to profusely thank Andrew Birkin for his advice and guidance on how to go about utilising the sources available to me, and for the unspoken support. Having written his own book on J.M. Barrie in the seventies, his response alone was incredibly flattering, and I wish him all the best with the charity he set up in memory of his son: Anno's Africa.

Thank you to the Walter Beinecke Rare Book and Manuscript Library at Yale University for providing the Llewelyn Davies Family Papers online, making available most of the letters, notes and photographs captured in this book. Although I was not in direct contact with them, their provision of these documents online saved a trip to the US, and I trust that if anything has been wrongly cited or acknowledged then they will reach out.

Thanks to Adam Reed from the Blair Partnership and Jenny from Great Ormond Street Children's Charity for their advice and assistance about the use of Barrie's work. Thanks are also owed to the National Trust Scotland, particularly the lovely staff at Barrie's Birthplace in Kirriemuir, for keeping such a historical landmark open to the public for more people to learn about Barrie and his roots.

Most of the documents and photographs are without owners since the Barrie estate was wound up in 1987, and many of the owners are either no longer with us or have no further legacy, but I would still like to express gratitude to those individuals whose words are printed here. To Dolly Ponsonby and her family, Mary Ansell, Daphne du Maurier and her family, and of course the Llewelyn Davies family, including Laura Duguid and her contributions to help keep Barrie's most famous work alive, I give them all my thanks, regardless of the fact they will never know of this.

When it comes to the production of this book, I cannot thank Charlotte Mitchell enough for all her help in answering my endless questions, and helping with not only the marketing but also the copyright. Laura Hirst, who handled the production, also deserves my gratitude for being so patient with the nit-picky changes I requested to the layout, and thus presenting me with a beautiful book. Of course, I cannot forget to throw Jon Wilkinson into the mix, who designed a cover I couldn't have imagined to be any better; I was awestruck with the very first design. It matches Barrie perfectly.

Finally, to my partner, friends and family, thank you: I hope this explains why I was always so indulgent with the story of Peter Pan and its creator.

And of course, to Mr Barrie: thank you for creating the story that got me through childhood and, ironically, adulthood. I wish only that you will now be seen as the truly remarkable man that you were.

DISCLAIMER

Although all efforts were made to track down the rightful copyright owners to all source materials, many estates have no continued line or the material is in the public domain; if anyone feels they have not been consulted and the copyright is breached, then please be in touch so that the rightful owners can be credited for future editions.

I would also like to clarify that neither Great Ormond Street Hospital or any other individuals or corporations other than Pen and Sword are responsible for the contents or publication of this book.

Prologue

'May God blast anyone that writes a biography about me,'[1] should certainly be warning enough to stop the writing of any books that circle the life of Sir James Matthew Barrie, renowned author of the internationally loved story of *Peter Pan*.[2] This quote, which comes directly from him, is mentioned in most biographies – this one, too – almost as a plea for him to forgive the writer for being another person delving into every crevice of his private and public life. With such a fascinating background, and the creator of one of fiction's most well-known characters, he is almost impossible not to revisit. Over the years, he's been marked as a potential paedophile, manipulator, exploiter, a flirt and just plain strange, with most articles questioning his innocence and intentions; it's little wonder that I am another back at this door.

Primarily, I should point out that what I write here in opinion is not definitive fact. As much as I may believe in the theories presented, the life of Mr Barrie will forever remain under speculation due to a lack of concrete evidence. I've taken from the personal letters of many to paint as broad a picture as I can without sounding biased, and would also like to make clear that there is also no intention to offend anyone spoken about in this book; I only hope to shed light on a new perspective, one that I haven't seen published yet and was devised out of personal understanding and solidarity. After all, the character of Peter Pan is more than just a work of fiction; he is an embodiment of youth and the spirit of his author.

Any fiction writer will tell you that some of their characters were partly based on themselves, or others, and it's near-impossible to create something that hasn't been influenced by the personality and mannerisms of someone that actually exists. J.M. Barrie absolutely put parts of himself into the creation of The Boy Who Wouldn't Grow Up, which forces us to closely examine who he really was and why he acted in the way he did. His inspiration for *Peter Pan* is always put down to the stories he told the Llewelyn Davies children, boys he met in Kensington Gardens and befriended, but it really sparked as early as his childhood.

Facing so much grief and from such a young age in his life, the story of the magic and adventures in Neverland that we know and love actually originated from a place of sorrow and loss and, as a result, Barrie clung to the simplicity and joys of being a child.

Unlike similarly explored writers such as Lewis Carroll, whose activity with young girls throughout his life raises much more suspicion and speculation, the relationships that Barrie was able to develop with children came from a place of escapism from the adult world of high Edwardian society. That, and the probability that the Scottish playwright was probably the first person to knowingly suffer from Peter Pan Syndrome, a pop-psychology term attached to people who are socially immature. Most people that associate with it feel unable to accept the inevitability of growing up, taking refuge in the actions and thought processes of a child, and when we examine Barrie's behaviour throughout his life, it fits.

It's a cruel irony, to have created the character that inspired the term, and express signs of it himself.

Furthermore, the character of Peter is more complex than many might think. If we analyse the original Peter – Barrie's version of him – we see just how much The Walt Disney Company distorted such an interesting character to be much cleaner and innocent. Most adaptations since the 1953 cartoon have since depicted Peter to be nothing more than a child that likes to play games, have fun and can fly, basing off Disney's version rather than inspecting the original source. Movies and TV specials such as *Hook* (1990)[3], *Neverland* (2011)[4] and *Pan* (2015)[5] create a charming narrative but ultimately, miss the mark of Barrie's Peter, whose capability of cruelty is eradicated from most versions.

The adaptation that seems to best represent not only Peter but Wendy, Captain Hook and the other key characters of the story, is P.J. Hogan's *Peter Pan* (2003)[6]. Not only do we see Peter's inability to process or feel romantic feeling and emotion as Barrie portrayed him, but lots of features from the play (which actually came before the novel) were incorporated, such as the same actor playing Captain Hook and Mr Darling. A later analysis of key screen adaptations will cover this in more detail, which is once again subject to opinion.

Prologue

It comes back to the question in hand: who was James Barrie? A small, withdrawn man who preferred the company of children to any adult; a writer whose main work overshadowed all his others; a father-figure and guardian for children? Or was he truly a dark and sinister man that kept to the shadows, a creature of ominous intent with little to no regard for polite, adult society or the riches that he gained from his success?

In the words of Nico Llewelyn Davies, it is left to the mind to wonder if Barrie was indeed 'an innocent', incapable of inappropriate feelings or anything resembling romantic feeling, or if there lays hidden a truth that none are left alive to share.

Chapter 1

All children, except one, grow up 1860–1878

Born the ninth of ten children, James Matthew Barrie had humble beginnings in Kirriemuir, Angus, Scotland. His father was a hand-loom weaver and his mother ran the house, and in this way little James's arrival on 9th May 1860 was not seen as a particularly special occasion when it had all been done so many times before. He was treated just like the others, encouraged to pursue an education and an academic career rather than pushed into work as early as possible, being taught the 'three R's', (reading, writing and arithmetic). Nothing much appeared special about him, save for his exceptionally small stature.

In his early years, the young James Barrie would've grown up on a number of folktales common to the Perthshire area, witches being the centre of most stories around his birthplace. Other stories included mischievous elves and fairies and water sprites; *The Urisk of Monless Burn*[1] tells of an urisk (a pixie-like creature, generally known as a brownie) that helped a farmer's crops grow in return for a daily receiving of milk and buns. Another tale that originated from Fife – a little further from Barrie's birthplace – is *The Fairy Boy of Leith*,[2] which is about a boy that played the drums for the elves and fairies of a hill near his village. This one could've had particular influence on his most famous work yet to come considering the link between Peter Pan and the fairies.

Kirriemuir, the burgh Barrie lived in with his family, was a dwelling surrounded by the Scottish countryside where many of these tales were birthed. With fantastical brooks and surrounding hills full of mystery, it was easy for residents to fabricate stories, creatures and characters that would be hiding around them. With such a rich pool of inspiration to take from, it's unsurprising that the young James was able to develop the creative

The Dark Side of Peter Pan

imagination that led to his own writing. In his later collection, *A Window in Thrums*,[3] he wrote of Kirriemuir:

> *'To those who dwell in great cities Thrums is only a small place, but what a clatter of life it has for me.'*[4]

His mother, Margaret Ogilvy was the main teller of these early stories, and Barrie's primary influence into literature. In his biography of her, *Margaret Ogilvy*,[5] he wrote:

> *'We read many books together when I was a boy. 'Robinson Crusoe' being the first (and the second), and the 'Arabian Nights' should have been the next, for we got it out of the library (a penny for three days), but on discovering that they were nights when we had paid for knights we sent that volume packing, and I have curled my lips at it ever since... Besides reading every book we could hire or borrow I also bought one now and again, and while buying (it was the occupation of weeks) I read, standing at the counter, most of the other books in the shop, which is perhaps the most exquisite way of reading.'*[6]

From here, Barrie developed the fondness for storytelling, which Margaret encouraged:

> *'...but on a day I conceived a glorious idea, or was it put into my head by my mother, then desirous of making progress with her new clouty hearthrug. The notion was nothing short of this, why should I not write the tales myself? I did write them – in the garret – but they by no means helped her to get on with her work, for when I finished a chapter I bounded downstairs to read it out to her, and so short were the chapters, so ready was the pen, that I was back with a new manuscript before another clout was added to the rug... They were all tales of adventure (happiest is he who writes of adventure), no characters were allowed within if I knew their like in the flesh, the scene lay in unknown parts, desert islands, enchanted gardens, with knights (none of your nights) on black chargers...'*[7]

All children, except one, grow up

Young James was very fond of his mother and formed a deep bond with her that lasted for the rest of her life. He was fascinated by the stories she had to tell, not just folktales that circulated the town but tales of her own childhood. At the age of eight, Margaret had taken over the household from her recently-passed mother, and was forced to step out of childhood and into the shoes of responsibility to help with running the house in her mother's stead. In her later years as a mother, she relived her lost childhood through her own children, particularly James.

Barrie seemed to find comfort in his mother's loss of a childhood, in that he too was afraid of leaving his own behind. He wrote in *Margaret Ogilvy*:

> '*The horror of my boyhood was that I knew a time would come when I also must give up the games, and how it was to be done I saw not… I felt that I must continue playing in secret, and I took this shadow to her, when she told me her own experience, which convinced us both that we were very like each other inside.*' [8]

Despite this bond, the young storyteller was living in the shadow of his older brother – and his mother's obvious favourite child – David. Handsome, charming, athletic and intelligent, he was the golden child, showing potential to become a Minister. Being so small and not particularly striking in appearance, little James couldn't match up.

And the concept of not leaving childhood behind soon took on a new perspective when David was killed in an ice-skating accident in January 1867, on the eve of his fourteenth birthday. James was six.

He didn't remember much from the event, only playing with his younger sister Maggie under the table on which David's coffin stood, proof that being exposed to grief at such a young age was most likely a numb experience for him, especially when it was the brother whose shade he struggled to break free from.

In *A Window in Thrums*, Barrie did at least come to reflect on this time and the effect the death had on those around him by fictionalising the situation. He writes clearly of grief:

> '*…then came the terrible moment… the moment known to shuddering watchers by sick beds, when a chill wind cuts*

> *through the house, and the world without seems cold in death. It is as if the heart of the earth did not mean to continue beating.*[9]

David's death would continue to follow Barrie throughout his life, despite his brother's presence being no longer physical.

As a result of David's death, Margaret retreated into her despair and became quite ill. She remained bedbound, inconsolable, and lost in her depression. Barrie recalled going into her bedroom:

> *'...the room was dark, and when I heard the door shut and no sound came from the bed I was afraid, and I stood still. I suppose I was breathing hard, or perhaps I was crying, for after a time I heard a listless voice that had never been listless before, say 'Is that you?' I think the tone hurt me, for I made no answer, and then the voice said more anxiously 'Is that you?' again. I thought it was the dead boy she was speaking to, and I said in a little lonely voice, 'No, it's no him, it's just me.' Then I heard a cry, and my mother turned in bed, and though it was dark I knew that she was holding out her arms.'*[10]

For a mere boy of six, his understanding of the world and his places in it is heart-wrenching; he was fully aware that David had been his mother's favourite. Any child would despair to acknowledge such a truth.

From that time onwards, Barrie's devotion to his mother was shown through his determination to bring her some joy. He spent most of his time sitting on her bed with her, telling stories and doing his best to bring out her laughter.

> *'...my anxiety to brighten her gave my face a strained look and put a tremor into the joke... I kept a record of her laughs on a piece of paper, a stroke for each, and it was my custom to show this proudly to the doctor every morning.'*[11]

It became his personal task to sit with her every day, telling stories and funny anecdotes 'trying to make her forget him'. At times he of course became hurt by the love she had for a boy that was no longer there, crying out to her, 'Do you mind nothing about me?' A child of six years old couldn't comprehend the pain she was experiencing, only feeling that he wasn't enough in his brother's absence, but wanted to provide love and happiness to her nonetheless.

> 'A good woman who suffers is altogether beyond man's reckoning. To such heights of self-sacrifice we cannot rise.'[12]

He went on to explain in his mother's biography:

> 'I have heard no such laugh as hers save from merry children; the laughter of most of us ages, and wears out with the body, but hers remained gleeful to the last, as if it were born afresh every morning.'[13]

Perhaps this was one of the key reasons why he came to love the company of children so much: hearing his own mother's laugh within theirs, trying to grasp the memory of her in any way he possibly could.

It would explain why Margaret makes so many appearances in future characters when they are inspected. He spent his career bringing his mother forth in fiction, and later back to life through his writing, in particular through the character of Wendy Darling.

There are a number of clues written by Barrie about Margaret that heavily suggest early inspiration for Wendy, including his note that 'blue was her colour' and her general motherly nature being pressed upon the fictional. In her later years, Margaret became known to look for herself in his stories, knowing she was bound to be there somewhere:

> '"...he tries to keep me out, but he canna; it's more than he can do!"'[14]

In fact, it seemed that his mother's approval mattered so much to him that other aspects of his writing were also affected:

> '...my mother did not care for scenery, and that is why there is so little of it in my books.'[15]

Whilst Wendy's character stemmed from one person, developed from a place of knowing, understanding and care, Peter Pan's character comes from a darker, complicated place, born from the tragedy that befell Margaret in losing her favourite son. In the depths of her despair, the young James often dressed up in his deceased brother's clothes and did his best to adopt his mannerisms in order to bring some comfort to his mother.

Instead, the comfort she was afforded was the simple fact that David 'would remain a boy forever'. As they all continued to grow older, he would be frozen in time at the age of thirteen. Barrie wrote:

> *'When I became a man... he was still a boy of thirteen...'*[16]

That was the beginning of Peter. The fully fledged idea of him, however, wasn't to manifest for a few decades more, remaining dormant throughout the remainder of his childhood. Peter's character is most-often described as being around the age bracket of thirteen, a bit of a coincidence since that's the age David's life was cut short; just on the cusp of fourteen and the beginning of adolescence.

Time passed, and although Margaret got physically better and soon left the confines of her bed and bedroom, the shadow of David remained over James. And no doubt her grief had left its mark as well, sparking ideas in a young boy's head that would form together over the years to become one of the greatest stories ever written.

> *'I daresay that when night comes, this Hyde Park which is so gay by day, is haunted by the ghosts of many mothers, who run, wild-eyed, from seat to seat, looking for their sons.'*[17]

In 1873, at the age of thirteen, Barrie attended Dumfries Academy, where his literary interests were gently forced into submission for a few years. This was a place more inclined in physical sport rather than the written word, so the young James took to football and fishing expeditions to fit in with the interests of his peers. Despite his childhood naturally (and sadly) having come to an end here, (for 'nothing that happens after we are twelve matters very much'[18]), he described the five years he spent at Dumfries Academy as 'the best of his life'.

This was perhaps owed to the friendship he formed with Stuart Gordon, though he was nicknamed 'Dare Devil Dick'. They used to play pirates together in the gardens of Moat Brae, continuing the games that Barrie was so afraid of having to leave behind. He later recollected in a speech he made at Dumfries Academy in 1924:

> *'For our escapades in a certain Dumfries garden, which is enchanted land to me, were certainly the genesis of that nefarious work* [Peter Pan]. *We lived in the tree-tops, on coconuts attached thereto, and that were in a bad condition; we were buccaneers and I kept the log-book of our depredations, an eerie journal... I should like one last look in it, to see if Captain Hook is in it.'*

Having such a friendship with another boy that also appeared to be quite content staying in his childhood a little longer too must've been the biggest comfort to Barrie, such that helped him become more confident as a young and impressionable pupil.

Barrie helped to form the school magazine where his love of writing finally made its reappearance; *Recollections of a School Master*, his first published story, was released in one of the issues. It reignited his passion for storytelling, and his chosen form of prose soon developed into scripts for the stage.

Visits to the theatre at Dumfries led Barrie to write his first ever play at the age of fifteen: *Bandalero the Bandit*, which has no remaining pages to this day. Despite it being marked as a 'grossly immoral play' by one disgruntled clergyman, it was a gateway review that caught the attention of a handful of London newspapers. The controversy, being the two villains in the play just acting like most other villains in a good story, caused a little fame to be dropped on Barrie in the school corridors. It was almost like a foreshadowing of the future his career would bring for him.

However, becoming a celebrity amongst his peers only seemed to make him feel a failure; although popular amongst the boys, the girls only appeared to find him endearing, something he did not find flattering. He wrote in one of his personal notebooks:

> *'- The boys write on walls, &c, name of boy and girl, coupling them together. As never did it to me. I wrote my own with girl's name.'*[19]

Barrie's height was becoming a barrier for him, throwing him back to the days just before he left home to attend Dumfries, the final days of his boyhood. He later wrote in a letter dated 21st December 1931:

> *'Six feet three inches… If I had really grown to this it would have made a great difference in my life. I would not have bothered turning out reels of printed matter. My one aim would have been to become a favourite of the ladies which between you and me has always been my sorrowful ambition. The things I could have said to them if my legs had been longer.'* [20]

Girls didn't really interest Barrie in the way they seemed to interest his male peers, though he tried to make it so: writing his name alongside a girl he knew of (in a practice commonly seen over hundreds of years) was perhaps more out of obligation – it's what his peers were doing – or desperation to fit in, but any kind of feeling was never involved. It's easily suggestible at this point that Barrie was asexual, for he harboured no apparent feelings for the boys, either.

Asexual: a person who experiences little or no sexual attraction to other people.

As we look through the rest of his life, it's the most fitting description of the playwright regarding sexuality, who projected those feelings (or lack thereof) onto Peter Pan. More evidence of this will be explored in later chapters.

By the time he was seventeen years old, Barrie was only just 5ft. and didn't yet need to shave. Being so small, looking so young still, was something that affected him even though he battled with wanting to remain a child. He wrote in his personal notebook:

> *'-Ashamed at being small enough to travel half ticket by rail.'* [21]

He didn't feel as if he belonged, that his moments of celebrity in school only put the spotlight on him being so different and outcast, rather than highlighting his talent and potential. All this just as he was finding a place amongst people that he felt himself around.

All children, except one, grow up

In 1878, at the age of eighteen, Barrie returned to his home in Kirriemuir with the dream and intention of becoming a writer. He expressed this to his parents, but Margaret had other plans for him. She hinted how David, her lost son, would've gone to university had he lived, and the willing-to-please James was encouraged to attend himself. Once again, the shadow of his older brother was dictating his life, his mother looking for her dead son in her youngest. Barrie headed off to the University of Edinburgh but at a compromise: he was going to study Literature.

It must be noted that throughout the reminiscence of his childhood, Barrie's father rarely makes an appearance. This wasn't because he was absent or deceased or uncaring; his lack of mention was most likely due to the time period's perception of fatherhood, which is a common theme that affected Barrie's life and relationships to come. Barrie said of his father:

'...a man I am very proud to be able to call my father...' [22]

In the Victorian era, fathers did not show affection towards their sons – to do so was considered odd – and Mr David Barrie Sr. and his own son James were no different. Although Barrie's love for his mother was strong and written of endlessly, this was seen as nothing more or less than devotion between a mother and son, but such adoration between a father and son was for some reason frowned upon in that society.

This issue of affection between men – even men that were biologically related – was to remain apparent throughout Barrie's life.

Chapter 2

I don't want ever to be a man
1878–1884

Robert Galloway, a student at the University of Edinburgh, observed a lone figure walking the halls of the grand school.

> '[He was] exceedingly shy and diffident, and I do not remember ever to have seen him either enter or leave a classroom with any companion… I remember him distinctly – a sallow-faced, round-shouldered, slight, somewhat delicate-looking figure, who quietly went in and out amongst us, attracting but little observation, but himself observing all and measuring up men and treasuring up impressions.'[1]

He was, of course, observing James Barrie, a Literature student who enrolled at the university in 1878. The young man didn't join any clubs or societies and didn't have many – if any – friends.

Perhaps it was a childish rebellion against his parents, who'd pushed for him to attend university and head down the career path of a minister rather than indulge in dreams of becoming a creator of the arts. Most likely, however, it was just in his nature to be a wallflower.

His deceased brother David's shadow cast itself from Kirriemuir all the way to Edinburgh, where Barrie spent the days locked away in his room to study, write, and make observations of those around him. A prior discussion with his brother, Alexander, may have led to a compromise to study Literature, but no deals were made about a social aspect. In that respect, he was as far from becoming his brother David as he could get.

As a result, there isn't much of a record of Barrie's life at university, save for the writings in his personal notebooks; he watched his peers around him and wrote about this new world that was vastly different – and bigger – than the small burgh he'd come from.

In one of his observations, he wrote:

> '*-Far finer and nobler things in the world than loving a girl and getting her*
> *-Greatest horror – dream that I am married – wake up shrieking.*'[2]

Once again facing the world of boys being captivated by girls, Barrie found himself completely uninterested and excluded. The idea of his life holding nothing more than finding female companionship and signing the contract of marriage was a confusing sentiment to him; he believed in a world where there was so much more than what he could see his peers were all captivated by.

Women seemed to puzzle him, and his lack of attraction to them leads to the question of asexuality. He felt nothing sexual or romantic for them, and there is no evidence in his personal notebooks to him feeling any attraction towards his fellow sex, either, even at the ages of 18 to 22 where it was all his friends seemed capable of discussing.

> '*I lived too much in my art, and my solitary thoughts. I shrank from men's free talk of women, and yet when I left them it was to brood of the things they spoke of.*'[3]

These lines from *The Wedding Guest* suggest that it frustrated him that he was unable to feel excited by the same topics as his peers and was confused about why this was.

It's probably why he reveled in the thought processes and delights of childhood so much: being a child is to believe that anything is possible, and the denial of dreams considered a cruelty to those that haven't experienced enough of the world or of life yet.

He further wrote in his private notes:

> '*-Grow up & have to give up marbles – awful thought*
> *-Want to go into shop and buy brooch for child, but don't dare.*'[4]

Slipping so quickly and suddenly away from the best years of his life, this is a theme he continued to return to. To stay young, to keep playing was his escape from the monotony of adult life, as well as the restrictions that his parents established in presenting only a tunnel-vision of his future to become a minister.

At least in all his time at university he could still rely on the solace of writing. Alongside his studies, Barrie wrote drama reviews for the *Edinburgh Evening Courant*. His desire to become an author lived on, no matter what kind of lifestyle he was being steered towards, and his determination to pursue this path despite no apparent support around him is admirable.

After graduating from the University of Edinburgh with an M.A. on 21st April 1882, Barrie once again found himself returning home to Kirriemuir. In the years he was gone, his mother had hoped that he would 'grow out' of his dream to pursue a career in writing; maybe his time in a city and amongst his supposedly like-minded peers would guide him towards a more academic career? Alas, this was not the case with the young James feeling excluded from his peers nonetheless.

And James was persistent. He was not his brother, David.

Eventually, when it was clear that his parents' wishes for him would not come to pass, it was his sister Jane Ann that showed him an advertisement in *The Scotsman* for a leader-writer on the *Nottingham Journal*, a provincial newspaper. Barrie applied and was offered the post for £3 a week, which is approximately £292 in 2023.

His column was quipped with wit and what many now refer to as 'Barrie-esque humour', which many readers struggled to resonate with at the time. After a year-and-a-half with them, his employment with the *Nottingham Journal* ended in October 1884.

Barrie was not perturbed, however. He took this opportunity to start pushing his writing into the wider world, hounding London publications for a job with his articles. He sent numerous stories in an 'Auld Lichts' series, which were based on Margaret Ogilvy's recollections of Kirriemuir from her childhood. These included *An Auld Licht Community*, *An Auld Licht Funeral* and *An Auld Licht Scandal*. The *St James Gazette* published the first one on 17th November 1884.

The Gazette's editor, Frederick Greenwood, was fond of 'that Scotch thing' and his enthusiasm for receiving the endearing stories encouraged

Barrie to make the risky move to London in order to catch his opportunity while it still blazed:

> *'I wrote and asked the editor if I should come to London, and he said No, so I went, laden with charges from my mother to walk in the middle of the street... never to venture forth after sunset, and always to lock up everything... London, which she never saw, was to her a monster that licked up country youths as they stepped from the train...'*[5]

With no affirmative answer but confidence in his pocket, Barrie packed himself up and took the night-train to London, much to his mother's dismay. She feared for him, as any mother would; her small boy – now a man in all ways despite the illusion his height created – was heading into the pits of the big city, the jaws of the crocodile, even. Whether Barrie felt any nerves to his move is unrecorded, but he later wrote in *A Window in Thrums*:

> *'In the lustiness of youth there are many who cannot feel that they, too, will die.'*[6]

It was 1884, and the Scotsman dived in among the English.

Chapter 3

There is something she wants to be to me, but she says it is not my mother 1884–1897

At full height, Barrie was only 5ft 3½ inches. A small man in a large crowd could easily have become swept up in the human monsoon that was London, and yet the young writer quickly established himself in his trade; in his first three years of living there, he'd contributed to almost every notable publication there was.

One of these was the *National Observer*, whom Rudyard Kipling (author of *The Jungle Book*[1]) and H.G. Wells (author of *The War of The Worlds*[2]) were also known to submit pieces to, but on the side Barrie's dream to become a novelist was slowly taking a more refined form. Journalism was an easy way for him to earn a living, with articles and stories going out all across the country, but it was not enough to satisfy him.

His first novel, *Better Dead*, was published in 1888, which took on a more formal tone than his casual writings for local publications; and it appeared to be too formal for the public, who struggled to warm to it. Since Barrie had covered the expenses of printing it himself, he ended up losing £25 to the rejected book, which is the equivalent to almost £2,300 today according to 2023 inflation rates.

This did not deter him, however. He went on to compile his 'Auld Licht' stories, previously written for the *St James Gazette*, into a book, calling it *Auld Licht Idylls*. This was published in April 1888, and quickly followed up with a sequel: *A Window in Thrums*. Both titles were received with much more enthusiasm, praising Barrie's 'streak of sentimentality'. He'd tried to gain his success by blending in and doing as the other famous writers did, but standing out so uniquely was the very thing that his readership was after.

There is something she wants to be to me, but she says it is not my mother

The third collection in the series, *The Little Minister*, was published in 1891, and by this time Barrie's writings had reached not just all corners of the UK but also across the Atlantic and into the United States as well. His growing popularity and readership helped him to form a friendship with Robert Louis Stevenson (author of *Treasure Island*) and the two shared a great many letters over the years. Stevenson was a writer that Barrie greatly admired, and coincidentally that his mother also greatly admired, though she tried to hide it.

Margaret Ogilvy was quite clearly concerned that her love for Robert Louis Stevenson's writings, particularly his novel *Treasure Island*, would diminish the pride she had in her son and his own stories. She was particularly sensitive to how he might feel at the prospect of her being more a fan of a writer different to her own son, which may suggest she was aware of how her eldest, David, had overshadowed Barrie in the past:

> 'But how enamoured she was with 'Treasure Island', and how faithful she tried to be to me all the time she was reading it! I had to put her hands over her eyes to let her know that I had entered the room, and even then she might try to read between my fingers, coming to herself presently, however, so say 'It's a haver of a book.'
>
> "Those pirate stories are so uninteresting,' I would reply without fear, for she was too engrossed to see through me. 'Do you think you will finish this one?'
>
> "I may as well go on with it since I have begun it,' my mother says, so slyly that my sister and I shake our heads at each other to imply, 'Was there ever such a woman!'
>
> "There are none of those one-legged scoundrels in my books,' I say.
>
> "Better without them,' she replies promptly.
>
> "I wonder, mother, what is it about the man that so infatuates the public?'
>
> "He takes no hold of me,' she insists. 'I would a handle rather read your books.'...
>
> '... I remember how she read... holding it close to the ribs of the fire (because she could not spare a moment to rise and light the gas), and how, when bed-time came, and we coaxed,

> *remonstrated, scolded, she said quite fiercely, clinging to the book, 'I dinna lay my head on a pillow this night till I see how that laddie got out of the barrel.'*[3]

It was another endearing act that his mother did to make him worship her so.

Meanwhile, Barrie's interest in the theatre was making a return to the surface by 1891, where his appearances on the sets made him known for being flirtatious with a number of the young female actresses. It was as if, finally, he understood the fun of chasing girls that he'd missed out on in his years at Dumfries Academy and Edinburgh University. Perhaps his previous non-existent desire to catch the attentions of women were simply delayed?

His flirtations spread through actresses such as Minnie Palmer, Phyllis Broughton and Irene Vanbrugh etc. He wrote in his personal notes of that year:

> *'-...He always wanted to kiss pretty girls tho' manner made him stiff with them... Thus missed flirting days of boyhood and they came later when he knew the world*
> *-Had he even a genuine deep feeling that wasn't merely sentiment? Was he capable of it? Perhaps not.'*[4]

We can only guess from this that he wanted to love in the romantic sense he witnessed in others but seemed incapable of feeling it, hence his flirtations never seeming to last long. Though he could have felt the spark of something in flirting with such women, never getting past this stage was most likely a sentiment of no true feeling being behind it. It's very similar to how Peter Pan's character was written out.

At the beginning of *Peter and Wendy* (modernly printed as *Peter Pan*), Peter describes Tinker Bell:

> *"'She is not very polite. She says you are a great ugly girl, and that she is my fairy.'"*[5]

It's clear throughout the story that Tink's jealousy of Wendy is due to a love for Peter, but Peter cannot comprehend romantic love. He even states of Tiger Lily later in the book:

There is something she wants to be to me, but she says it is not my mother

> [To Wendy] *"You are so queer... and Tiger Lily is just the same. There is something she wants to be to me, but she says it is not my mother."* [6]

It's a trait that Barrie seemed to let flow into Peter, the Boy Who Wouldn't Grow Up... or Couldn't?

In 1892, Barrie's second play went into rehearsal in the spring. *Walker, London* was a comedy, in which a holidaying family are taken in by a barber, who pretends to be of a higher class than them. For a while it lacked a second leading lady, and in his search for the right person, Barrie asked his friend Jerome K. Jerome if he knew of anyone, 'young, beautiful, quite charming, a genius for preference, and able to flirt.' These were requirements that would clearly suit not only the role she'd be filling but his own personal desires.

Jerome came back with the suggestion of Mary Ansell, who ran her own touring company. She was young, pretty, and seemed to tick all the Scottish playwright's requirements. Upon meeting her, Barrie almost immediately offered her the part, which tossed Irene Vanbrugh to one side, who had initially been the actress up for the role.

In later years, Vanbrugh stated that 'the author was in love with her', in reference to Barrie and Ansell. It seemed that most women were not eluded to the use Barrie's charm had on them.

His ability to toss people aside for the latest plaything was one of his most childish traits, and it only adds to the theory of Barrie being the first recorded example of someone that showed symptoms of Peter Pan Syndrome. Immaturity often seemed to crop up in various situations with adults, spotlighting him amongst his peers.

It was no wonder then that his continued flirtations with Mary Ansell came to attract the press. They were fascinated by the playwright and the actress – it was like something straight out of a story – circling them in the following months and leaving hints that a proposal must be on the horizon.

And yet, Barrie held off. His personal notes in the spring and summer of 1892 read:

> '-This sentimentalist wants to make girl love him, bullies and orders her... yet doesn't want to marry.

> *-Her ordering clothes for him, &c – Motherly feelings.'*
> *-His kindliness (weak), he feels for her & keeps the thing going on because doesn't want to make her miserable.*
> *-The man reflecting in his own mind as to whether he shd marry her – pros and cons – his pleasures in mild love with many girls to which his position has at last given him an entrance, they admire his work so much – He feels absolutely that married life wd be insupportable...* [7]

He enjoyed the thrill of the chase, and the idea of the capture made him despair.

It also has to be noted that his personal notes suggest he saw Ansell almost as a motherly figure, which was a trait that Peter Pan struggled with when it came to Wendy. Barrie knew and understood the kind of love he had for his mother and didn't correlate that what he might feel for Ansell should be of a different nature. Meanwhile, Peter Pan refers to Wendy as 'mother' throughout the story, not only to the Lost Boys but also to himself, despite being referred to as 'father' by the others.

Barrie's avoidance of a commitment to Ansell led him to flee London with his confused feelings. He headed back to his family in Kirriemuir, where his sister, Maggie, was due to marry.

Just before the wedding took place, he gifted the future husband of his sister, James Winter, with a horse, which was seen as a gift of the wealthy. His family were seeing for the first time the enormity of his success, how no expense would be spared when it came to offering them the support and comforts they had rarely been able to afford themselves. Barrie was not ashamed to share his wealth and his attitude towards money rarely changed; he wrote in *A Window in Thrums:*

> *'Money may always be a beautiful thing. It is we who make it grimy.'* [8]

However, just days after the wedding between Maggie and her new husband, James Winter was thrown from the horse that Barrie had given him and as a result, killed.

Maggie was inconsolable, unable to even attend the funeral of her new husband. Despite feeling he'd escaped his complicated relationship with

> There is something she wants to be to me, but she says it is not my mother

Mary Ansell for a while, he returned to London with a deep sorrow for his mourning sister, whom he felt responsible for her loss. He had, after all, gifted the very horse that James had been thrown from.

Maggie eventually married the brother of her deceased husband a year after – Willie Winter – but nonetheless it appeared that Barrie was constantly followed by guilt and grief hereafter.

And there was no rest for him back in London. Society magazines and gossip columns were bringing the pressure down on him to announce an engagement between him and Ansell, a topic of conversation it was now difficult to avoid. Although he still harboured mixed feelings, James Barrie proposed to Mary Ansell in 1894, and she accepted.

They were married on Monday 9th July 1894, by a local minister in his parent's home, according to Scottish custom. He may have had some wealth by this time, but he didn't spare much of it for their nuptials. In the couple of days before the small ceremony took place, he wrote in his personal notebooks:

> '-Our love has brought me nothing but misery.
> -Must we instruct you in the mysteries of love-making?'[9]

They suggest that not only did the purpose of marriage and romantic love elude him, but the obvious consummation that was to follow was to continue to be an uncomfortable part of adulthood for him.

Soon after the wedding, Barrie and his new wife left for Switzerland for their honeymoon, where Mary later described it as a 'shock' to a friend; it has been suggested by some that the marriage was never consummated, though this can only be confirmed as a rumour at most. Mary no doubt felt a little neglected by her new husband, who had so devotedly spent his time with her before but now appeared completely uninterested in her, isolating himself. He wrote in his notebook at the time:

> '-Wife – Have you given me up? Have nothing to do with me?'[10]

At least, whilst there, the newlyweds were blessed with Porthos.

As a wedding present, Barrie gifted Mary with a St. Bernard puppy, who was named after the St. Bernard in George du Maurier's novel *Peter Ibbetson* – an amazing coincidence with what was to come.

George du Maurier, father of the well-known writer Daphne du Maurier, was one of Barrie's favourite authors, and he had a huge respect for his writing as well as the man behind it. Naming his dog after one of the characters is a practice that is still seen today among fans of certain stories and the characters in them.

Porthos was very much a receptacle for a child, and he travelled back to London with them once the honeymoon came to an end. Mary doted on him in this way, and later wrote in *Dogs and Men*:[11]

> '*Perhaps my love for dogs, in the beginning, was a sort of mother-love. Porthos was a baby when I first saw him: a fat little round young thing... When the dogs loved me, they did it without forethought or afterthought, because they couldn't help it. But men didn't love me unless they wanted to; unless I fitted in with their idea of me.*'

However, Porthos ended up becoming more attached to his master rather than his mistress. Barrie was his playmate, and according to Mary, the two had 'fearful wrestling matches' and 'ran races, in and out of the rooms, up and down the stairs...'

He became a companion that Barrie was rarely seen without, and when the three of them moved to their first house in March 1895, the playwright and his faithful canine became a well-known picture seen strolling through Kensington Gardens every day.

The house 133 Gloucester Road was situated just across from the gardens, and it was here that Barrie began working on his novel *Sentimental Tommy*,[12] which reflected and explored Barrie's own boyhood in Kirriemuir. It can be considered that the character of Tommy was an early version of what Peter Pan was to become, due to Tommy's longing to remain a child being a repetitive theme throughout the book.

When *Sentimental Tommy* was finished, Barrie took it home to his very old and frail mother to read to her; her approval was still vital for him to obtain. Margaret Ogilvy insisted that she was still more than physically capable and continued to do housework and the like despite her daughter's protests, who was also acting as her care-giver.

> '*...she would be up and doing, for though pitifully frail she no longer suffered from any ailment. She seemed so well*

There is something she wants to be to me, but she says it is not my mother

> *comparatively that I, having still the remnants of an illness to shake off, was to take a holiday in Switzerland, and then return to her...* '[13]

Barrie and Mary headed off to Switzerland straight from there, convinced that Margaret was well and healthy, in order to celebrate their first wedding anniversary in the summer of 1895. Porthos, of course, accompanied them.

Once again, however, the young playwright was to be faced with another hit of guilt and grief. He received a telegram two weeks on to say that his sister had died during the night, just hours after receiving a letter from her that all was well at home. Being three days away from home, Barrie left for Kirriemuir immediately, since nothing had been said of his mother in light of the shock of his sister's sudden passing.

> 'The news I got on reaching London was this: my mother did not understand that her daughter was dead, and they were waiting for me to tell her.'[14]

And yet when he finally reached Kirriemuir, ready to break the news, he was twelve hours too late: his mother had also died.

He learned the full extent from his father and the doctor that had been called to his sister's bedside:

> *'My sister awoke [that] morning with a headache. She had always been a martyr to headaches, but this one, like many another, seemed to be unusually severe. Nevertheless she rose and lit my mother's fire and brought up her breakfast, and then had to return to bed. She was not able to write her daily letter to me, saying how my mother was, and almost the last thing she did was to ask my father to write it, and not to let on that she was ill, as it would distress me. The doctor was called, but she rapidly became unconscious. In this state she was removed from my mother's bed to another. It was discovered that she was suffering from an internal disease. No one had guessed it. She herself never knew. Nothing could be done. In this unconsciousness she passed away, without knowing that she was leaving her mother.'*[15]

The Dark Side of Peter Pan

And as for Margaret Ogilvy:

> *'My timid mother saw the one who was never to leave her carried unconscious from the room, and she did not break down. She who used to wring her hands if her daughter was gone for a moment never asked for her again... They told her I was on my way home, and she said with a confidant smile, 'He will come as quick as trains can bring him.'... She said goodbye to them all, and at last turned her face to the side where her best-beloved had lain... and the last they heard were 'God' and 'love'...'*[16]

Barrie attended their funerals, both held on the same day, and witnessed the two being buried together. Considering the effect his mother had on his life, it was no wonder that Margaret Ogilvy's death was so difficult for him to deal with.

> *'I saw her lying dead, and her face was beautiful and serene. But it was the other room I entered first, and it was by my sister's side that I fell upon my knees... And now I am left without them, but I trust my memory will ever go back to those happy days, not to rush through them, but dallying here and there, even as my mother wanders through my books.'*[17]

When he finally returned to London with his wife and dog, Barrie set to work writing a biography dedicated to his mother, titled simply: *Margaret Ogilvy*. By revisiting his memories of her through his mourning, he published a beautiful ode to the woman, capturing not only what she was to him but also who she was as a person. He lived through Margaret's memories as if his own and continued to make her his 'hero' by installing many of her traits in future stories and characters to come, but most predominantly in Wendy Darling.

Whilst grieving his mother, the Barrie's took their first trip to America in 1896. It was there that the Scottish playwright met Charles Frohman, a Broadway producer that was known by many as the 'Beaming Buddha of

> There is something she wants to be to me, but she says it is not my mother

Broadway'. Barrie's new theatrical agent, Addison Bright, hoped that a meeting between the two would materialise a stage production of Barrie's novel, *The Little Minister*,[18] whilst Frohman was looking for the right play to place an actress he'd recently discovered: Maude Adams.

Barrie and Frohman conclusively struck up a very good friendship as they seemed to have a few things in common: they both adored their mothers (though both were now dead), and both loved children but had none of their own. Their friendship and working relationship led to a number of collaborations on Barrie's plays in the years to come, with Frohman bringing them to life on American stages.

Returning to London, Barrie began working on a sequel to *Sentimental Tommy*, titled *Tommy and Grizel*,[19] which seemed to have many reflections of his marriage to Mary Ansell.

> '"Grizel... I want to love you... you are the only woman I ever wanted to love, but apparently I can't. I have decided to go on with this thing because it seems best for you, but is it?... I think I can love you in my own way, but I thought I loved you in their way, and it is the only way that counts in this world of theirs. It does not seem to be my world...'[20]

It was as if he was blatantly saying through the form of fiction that he could not love romantically, though he wished he could. He felt a love for Mary that *he* understood but was not accepted in the eyes of others. He couldn't force the romantic love expected between a husband and wife.

To add to his inner turmoil, Barrie knew that Mary was more than aware of this. After being married for a while, he must've made himself clear to her, and what he could and could not give.

> 'She knew that, despite all he had gone through, he was still a boy, And boys cannot love. Oh, is it not cruel to ask a boy to love ?... He did not love her, "Not as I love him," she said to herself. "Not as married people ought to love, but in the other way he loves me dearly."... He was a boy who could not grow up.'[21]

Through everything, Mary Barrie remained passive in the background. It had been three years since her marriage to James, and the pair still remained childless in 1897 – an oddity in the Victorian era. She had Porthos to dote on, treating him as a child, but it was no secret that she longed for children, the one thing her husband could not seem to give her.

He could, however, make friends with endless amounts of children. One of their neighbours on Gloucester Road, Maurice Hewlett, had two children: Cecco and Pia. Four-year-old Cecco often accompanied Barrie and Porthos on their walks through Kensington Gardens, and this name is seen as one of the pirates later to appear in *Peter and Wendy*. It was common for Barrie to use the names of people he knew as characters in his books.

Another example of this was that of Margaret Henley, daughter of W.E. Henley, who owned the *National Observer*. She used to refer to Barrie as her 'fwendy' since she couldn't pronounce her 'r's, and this went on to inspire the name 'Wendy'. Before then, 'Wendy' was not a name that existed, and after the publication of Barrie's most famous play and story, it saw a popular rise in the amount of baby girls being named after her, peaking in the 1960s. Margaret Henley tragically passed away at the age of six.

It was on these walks through the gardens with Porthos that Barrie came across George and Jack Lewellyn Davies, five and four years old at the time, in 1897. And it was here that the story of Peter Pan, dormant for so many years, would finally start to take on life.

Chapter 4

There never was a simpler happier family until the coming of Peter Pan 1897–1900

Kensington Gardens was often full of children and their nurses, especially in the early afternoon hours when schools had just been let out for the day. Barrie came to know the young boys of the Llewelyn Davies family very well in these times, talking of adventurous and mystical things like pirates and fairies, but also grounding them with the subject of cricket. George and Jack were old enough to frolic with him, whilst Peter was only a baby, and tended to stay by the children's nurse, Mary Hodgson. Mary was subtly against Barrie from the start, believing him to be a bad influence on her charges.

One of the main reasons Barrie seemed to enjoy the company of the boys – along with other children – so much was the fact that there seemed to be no social pressure with them; he was prone to periods of silent contemplation, which most adult company found unnerving or rude. Not children, however, and not George and Jack. They wouldn't scorn him for it, and this probably made him feel as if he could be his true self when he was around them.

Pamela Maude was another child that was friends with Barrie at the same time, whose father Cyril Maude was actually rehearsing for *The Little Minister* play. She said of the playwright:

> '...the next moment he was telling us about fairies as if he knew all about them. He was made of silences, but we did not find these strange; they were so much part of him that they expressed him more than anything he could say... it seemed to us that his silences spoke loudly.'[1]

In the gardens, Barrie told made-up stories for George, Jack and Peter, new ones every single day that they were enchanted by. They seemed to see him as an equal. Not a grown-up, but one of them.

Barrie knew that he was not like the other adults, that he didn't fit in with them so well, and his outlet for being self-aware of it appeared through his writing. As he worked on *Tommy and Grizel*, the sequel to *Sentimental Tommy*, it is clear that the character of Tommy was modelled more and more on himself:

> *'...he was ever a boy, trying sometimes, as now, to be a man, [but] always when he looked round he ran back to his boyhood as if he saw it holding out its arms to him and inviting him to come back and play. He was so fond of being a boy that he could not grow up.'*

> *'...he thinks he can now be a boy forever; and he fears that if they catch him they will compel him to grow into a man, so he runs further from them into the wood and is running still, singing to himself because he is always to be a boy.'*[2]

He hated to be an adult so much that he avoided the company of other adults as much as possible, so much so that he rarely accepted any invitations to social occasions where he'd have no choice but to be amongst those grown-ups in the upper class society of London. There was no one there to tell fascinating stories to, and no one that would entertain his imaginative mind or be pleasantly amused by the topic of fairies.

He did, however, accept an invitation to a New Year's Eve dinner party to personally celebrate his success as a playwright, both in England and in America; *The Little Minister* had opened on 27th September 1897 at Frohman's Empire Theatre in New York City – with Maude Adams as the star – and broke all Broadway records by running for over three hundred performances.

By this point, Barrie was still flirting with a number of the young actresses that he came across in his work in the theatre. His wife was more than likely aware that he did this, and disgruntled by it, but she was also all too aware of her husband's inability to take things further than the stage of flirting so she probably wasn't concerned; any thoughts she may have had on the subject are unrecorded. Their marriage therefore continued on in this manner.

There never was a simpler happier family until the coming of Peter Pan

The dinner party in question that Barrie decided to attend in good spirits was that of Sir George and Lady Lewis, the former being the best-known lawyer in London at the time. A number of other people from high society attended – seventy-two guests to be precise – including that of writers and artists, actors and musicians, lawyers and politicians etc. If Barrie felt a little out of place or out of his social depth upon his arrival to the large party, it didn't last too long.

One of these guests was Mrs Sylvia Llewelyn Davies, the wife of a young barrister: Arthur Llewelyn Davies. Barrie and Sylvia were seated next to each other at the table, and a conversation was struck up between them when Barrie noticed she was sneaking the after-dinner sweets into her silk handbag and asked her who they were for. She said they were 'for Peter', and it was quickly learnt after that that she was the mother of his friends in Kensington Gardens: little George and Jack and Peter.

As they talked, Barrie noted that she was 'the most beautiful creature he had ever seen', an insensitive thing to say about a woman who is not your wife, though to Barrie it was most likely an innocent remark he made without thinking. It's just as a child would do.

Their conversation continued, and it was then uncovered that Sylvia was, in fact, prior known as Sylvia du Maurier – the writer George du Maurier's daughter – George du Maurier, of course, being Barrie's favourite writer. Barrie excitedly regaled how his dog, Porthos, was named after the Saint Bernard in *Peter Ibbetson*,[3] whilst Sylvia countered this with the fact that her son Peter was named after the protagonist of the same book.

On the whole, the du Maurier's were an exceedingly successful family that even had links to royalty; George du Maurier's grandmother was mistress to Prince Frederick, Duke of York and Albany. George himself, having been born in Bohemian Paris, France, became a cartoonist for *Punch*, the British satirical magazine that spanned from 1841 to 2002, as well as a renowned writer that penned the famous novels *Peter Ibbetson* (1891) and *Trilby* (1895).[4] After marrying his wife, Emma, they had five children, including Sylvia and:

- Guy du Maurier, a Lieutenant Colonel in the English army and a playwright
- Gerald du Maurier, an actor that appeared on the stage as well as on film

Gerald's daughter, Daphne du Maurier, was also an extremely successful writer, authoring novels such as *Rebecca*[5] and *Jamaica Inn*,[6] as well as being a playwright and non-fiction writer. Gerald's other daughters were actress and novelist Angela du Maurier, and artist Jeanne du Maurier.

Furthermore, it can only be imagined Barrie's excitement at coming across one of the family himself, and none other than the mother of the boys he'd befriended in Kensington Gardens.

Now that Sylvia and Barrie had been introduced, he began to see a lot more of George, Jack and Peter. Not only did he see them at the usual times in the Gardens, but also at their home in 31 Kensington Gardens. By this time, Barrie and Sylvia's friendship was firmly set in stone, whilst her husband, Arthur Llewelyn Davies, reportedly remained more wary of him.

Predominantly, Arthur seemed confused by the small Scotsman. He could've felt threatened in the way many men would when another man started to become that close with his wife, as well as how much his sons were becoming to love him, but Barrie was clearly no threat. It was as if his marriage to Mary Ansell made it clear that he was incapable of feeling desire for women, and certainly wouldn't disrupt the marriage between Sylvia and Arthur.

In 1948, Peter Llewelyn Davies wrote to Mary Hodgson:

'It is clear enough that Father didn't like him, at any rate in the early stages.'[7]

Still, it was as if Barrie could flirt with Sylvia like he did with many of the young actresses in his productions, but be comforted by the knowledge that she would never act on it, being so happily married and devoted to her husband. His love for her was confusing to the people around them, considering that there was a lesser understanding of different kinds of love at the time and expressions of it, especially a platonic love between a man and a woman. Barrie loved Sylvia for the woman and mother that she was, with no extension upon that. No sexual or romantic attraction was involved, and perhaps watching her interactions with her sons reminded him of his own mother as well. After Margaret Ogilvy, Sylvia Llewellyn Davies was the epitome of motherhood.

There never was a simpler happier family until the coming of Peter Pan

Meanwhile, the boys were the epitome of childhood, more specifically boyhood.

Barrie was closest to George at this time and began developing a story titled *The Little White Bird*.[8] It encompassed a father/son type relationship between the two of them, and some of the notes pulled from his personal notebook includes:

> '- L.W.B. Telling George what love is… in answer to George's inquiries abt how to write a story.
>
> – L.W.B. What George said while walking me round the Round Pond (abt what to have for his birthday – ship – Greek armour – book &c) – I sneer.
>
> -The queer pleasure it gives when George tells me to lace his shoes.'[9]

Here, it's clear that Barrie did long to be a father, having suppressed paternal instincts and feelings that he entertained with George. In *The Little White Bird*, the character of the young boy David is heavily based off George, whilst Barrie narrates the story as the character Captain W, 'a gentle, whimsical, lonely old bachelor', (and also a writer that takes long walks in Kensington Gardens).

> 'He addresses me as father when he is in a hurry only, and never have I dared ask him to use the name. He says, "Come, Father," with an accursed beautiful carelessness. So let it be, David, for a little while longer.
>
> 'I like to hear him say it in front of others, as in shops… At such times the shopkeepers accept me as his father, and I cannot explain the particular pleasure this gives me. I am always in two minds then, to linger that we may have more of it [or] to snatch him away before he volunteers the information, "He is not really my father."'[10]

Barrie always wanted his own son, and he named the ghost of what could've been his son Timothy. Timothy made appearances within *The Little White Bird* but again, only as a possibility, not as a tangible character; the captain pretends to have a son that passed away, and when Barrie wrote of this, it was as if he was conveying to the world that it was the passing of his chance to become a biological father:

> *'...because he was not quite like other boys; and, so saying, he let go my finger and faded from before my eyes into another and golden ether; but I shall ever hold that had he been quite like other boys there would have been none braver than my Timothy.'*[11]

This is such a raw exposure of Barrie's inner turmoil of wanting to father a child that he didn't have to create himself with his wife, considering his ongoing issues with his own sexuality.

The visits with the Llewelyn Davies family continued; Barrie's life revolved around them. It was in this manner that the Lewellyn Davies family would become the basis for what was to be the fictional Darling family in *Peter Pan*.

Some days Barrie even picked the boys up from school and took them to Kensington Gardens, much to the disapproval of Mary Hodgson. She felt that her place as the children's nurse should've been firmly upheld as was tradition, and probably felt a little threatened by the playwright taking over her duties.

She duly became the inspiration for the nurse, Irene, in *The Little White Bird*:

> *'...we had become close friends, though the nurse was ever a threatening shadow in the background. Irene, in short, did not improve with acquaintance. I found her to be high and mighty, chiefly, I think, because she now wore a nurse's cap with streamers, of which the little creature was ludicrously proud. She assumed the airs of an official person, and always talked as if generations of babies had passed through her hands. She was also extremely jealous, and had a way of signifying disapproval of my methods that led to many coldnesses and even bickering between us, which I now see to have been undignified.'*[12]

At the same time, Barrie was working on *Tommy and Grizel*. It followed the relationship between the title character and Grizel, with her desire to

> There never was a simpler happier family until the coming of Peter Pan

marry countering Tommy's inability to mature. Barrie's infatuation with Sylvia went so far as to push her into the character of Grizel and his own wife out of it, whom the character was initially modelled. Grizel became more soft and gentle, much like the mother that Sylvia practiced being. Barrie even had a nickname for Sylvia that only he used – Jocelyn, her middle name.

Barrie's wife, Mary, didn't note her true opinions of him and the graceful Sylvia in any form. It's clear she must've been frustrated because she apparently became rather snobbish, most-likely in an attempt to vent her irritation; she was rude to staff and servants in the household and often bragged about Barrie's success and fortune, which he was disgruntled by. As a response, he set her on a mission to find a country home for them to spend the summers.

All the while, Barrie worked on *The Little White Bird*, a homage to his relationship with little George. The title derived from the idea that the little white birds are the birds that never find a mother; mothers and children were the pinnacle theme (one that Barrie didn't let go of in other projects), and whilst he and George wandered the gardens, the story unfolded from real life to on the page.

It eventually developed to include a new character named after George's little brother: Peter. Being just a baby at the time, Peter didn't get much of a say in the matter, which would later come to haunt him, but whilst being blissfully ignorant, George lapped up the story that Barrie spun for him. He said that all babies were once birds and would still try to fly away if it weren't for the bars on the nursery windows. George couldn't remember having ever been a bird, but Barrie insisted that he had just forgotten, that it was vital he forget, otherwise all children would fly away. It was originally told that Peter still tried to fly away, but George was skeptical – why then, did he always remain so still, so immobile in his pram? And so a second Peter was born: Peter Pan.

Barrie's choice of the name Peter had clear origins, whilst 'Pan' came from the Greek god Pan 'of the wild', who symbolised nature and was most often depicted as a piper. This is of course where the Pan Pipes got their name, and why Peter Pan is often portrayed as playing them.

Barrie told George that Peter Pan was a baby that had escaped the nursery and flew back to Kensington Gardens, specifically the island in the Serpentine where he came from. This island was inhabited by birds, and Peter lived there for some time among them as well as the fairies, not really belonging to either party:

> ' *"Then I shan't be exactly a human?" Peter asked.*
>
> ' *"No."*
>
> ' *"Nor exactly a bird?"*
>
> ' *"No."*
>
> ' *"What shall I be?"*
>
> ' *"You are a Betwixt-and-Between," Soloman said, and certainly he was a wise old fellow, for that is exactly how it turned out.'*[13]

Peter could fly but he wasn't a bird – so he was a child but he could fly.

Eventually, Peter felt a pull back to his mother, and decided to return to her. However, he was left heartbroken.

> '*...he flew straight to the window, which was always to be open for him.*
>
> '*But the window was closed, and there were iron bars on it, and peering inside he saw his mother sleeping peacefully with her arm around another little boy.*
>
> '*Peter called, "Mother! mother!" but she heard him not; in vain he beat his little limbs against the iron bars. He had to fly back, sobbing, to the gardens, and he never saw [her] again... When we reach the window it is Lock-out Time. The iron bars are up for life.'*[14]

Thus began Peter's vendetta against mothers, which is so against Barrie's own character. This is the beginning of demonstrating how Peter Pan was not meant to be a light and joyful character completely, but more like an anti-hero. Peter never lacked courage throughout his story, but his morals and understanding of many things are always distorted.

There never was a simpler happier family until the coming of Peter Pan

In 1899, *Tommy and Grizel* was finally published, though it was poorly received despite the anticipation after the success of the first in the duology. Perhaps Barrie wasn't so concerned about this when his writings took on a new passion and hyper-fixation – he couldn't keep away from the Llewelyn Davies boys when they brought him so much inspiration.

In August of the same year, the Llewelyn Davies family went on holiday to Rustington, a town on the South coast of England. And coincidentally, the Barrie's decided to holiday there too after returning from a trip to Germany, renting a house that was only half-a-mile from Sylvia and Arthur and their boys. Barrie was now able to spend full days with George, Jack and Peter, not taking into account that Arthur had finally been hoping to spend some quality time with his sons when his work kept him away from them all the rest of the year.

Barrie was likely not conscious of this in the same way a child might be: not considerate of those around him because those thought-processes just hadn't developed. His devotion to the boys wouldn't cause him to purposefully scorn their father – their real father – and even if it had been taken so, Arthur's thoughts on the matter aren't recorded. In later letters, he only had kind words to say of the Scotsman.

Back in London as the weather grew colder, the boys settled into a new school year and the origin story of Peter Pan continued to build. After establishing that Peter was neither entirely a human nor entirely a bird, he transcended into the status of a playful kind of spirit after a walk with George through Kensington Gardens. He pointed out to 'Jimmy' (the boys' name for him, which gradually became 'Uncle Jimmy') the boundary stones that mark the parish boundaries within the gardens, marked. 'W ST. M' and '13a. P.P. 1841'. They establish the border between the Parish of Westminster St Mary's and the Parish of Paddington. When George went on to ask what they were for, Barrie spun the story that when Peter Pan found dead children in the gardens after Lock-Out time, he would dig a grave and bury them, engraving a stone to mark the spot. Since children were known to die a lot in the Victorian era, it was a comfort to many to know what Peter Pan did for their spirits when he came across them:

> '...[Peter] went part of the way with them, so that they should not be frightened.'[15]

George found this wholly charming, and in response to the idea of flying with Peter Pan, the famous quote was born:

'To die will be an awfully big adventure.' [16]

In 1900, Sylvia fell pregnant with her fourth child, and Barrie seemed the most excited out of all of them since it would be the first child whose life he'd be a part of since birth – almost as if it were his own son whose birth he was sharing in.

It seemed apparent at this point that he would not be preparing for his own potential children at all, much as Mary wanted them. She was left to dote on Porthos the dog alone, and undertake the task Barrie had set her of finding a house to spend the summers. As everyone awaited the birth of Sylvia's next child, it was strange for others around the family to witness the small playwright spend more time with the family than his own wife, who must've felt more than a little neglected by her husband.

On the 16th June, Sylvia gave birth to Michael, the Llewelyn Davies boy that was soon to become Barrie's clear favourite; he was doted on by 'Uncle Jimmy' from the start.

Meanwhile, Mary Ansell had just found a country home for herself and Barrie in the April, which could only be reached down one country lane and surrounded by a pine forest. She set about renovating and decorating it, a project that kept her busy and distracted from the neglect she felt from her husband, though she made sure to reserve a large upstairs room with equally large windows as Barrie's study.

This country home was known as Black Lake Cottage.

Chapter 5

Come away, come away!
1901–1904

Black Lake Cottage was located in Farnham, Surrey. It's still there today but known under a new name. As given away by its original title, a lake lay nearby to the house – known as the Black Lake – which Barrie would make into oceans and lagoons for the Llewelyn Davies boys.

At the end of July in 1901, the Llewelyn Davies family rented a cottage in Tilford, which happened to be only a five-minute walk from the Barries' at Black Lake Cottage. The whole summer lay before Barrie to entertain the boys with stories of fairies and pirates and natives, exploring with them all around the lake.

With the eldest boy, George, heading off to school that September, Barrie knew he was on the cusp of losing him to a world that encouraged growing up and shaping boys into men. As well as this, Barrie would be losing his best friend to other boys of George's own age. Oliver Bailey made his appearance in *The Little White Bird* and was a clear representation for this, when the character of David was set to go off to Pilkington's Preparatory School (a play on the very real Wilkington's):

' *"He wants you not to call him Oliver any longer."*
' *"What shall I call him?"*
' *"Bailey."*
' *"But why?"*
' *"He's going to Pilkington's. And he can't play with us any more after next Saturday."*
' *"Why not?"*
' *"He's going to Pilkington's."*

> '*So now I knew the law about the thing, and we moved on together, Oliver stretching himself consciously, and methought that even David walked with a sedater air.*
>
> ' *"David," said I, with a sinking, "are you going to Pilkingson's?"*
>
> ' *"When I am eight," he replied.*
>
> ' *"And I shan't call you David then, and won't you play with me in the Gardens any more?"*
>
> '*He looked at Bailey, and Bailey signaled him to be firm.*
>
> ' *"Oh, no," said David cheerily.*
>
> '*Thus sharply did I learn how much longer I was to have him. Strange that a little boy can give so much pain.*'[1]

This is probably why Barrie was so determined to make the summer at Black Lake Cottage a resolutely fun and adventurous one for the boys.

The mixture of fairies, pirates and desert islands was to cater for all the boys in their games and stories, as the older two wanted more danger and risk whilst the young Peter still enjoyed the fancifulness of fairies. Michael, still a baby and too young to participate in the games at the time, would sit out until later summers.

Among the story telling and games played all around the lake, Barrie took a number of photographs of George and Jack and Peter. Many sported Porthos too, in roles as their protector and even as a tiger in a papier-mâché mask. Looking at them, it is clear that all were fully immersed in the games; Barrie himself played a pirate character called Captain Swarthy, an early draft of what would become Captain Hook, as some would consider.

When the photographs were developed later, the playwright incorporated them into a book he had professionally printed that he called *The Boy Castaways of Black Lake Island*,[2] of which just two copies were produced. Barrie later described this collection in his Dedication to *Peter Pan* as 'a now melancholy volume'; missing the past where youth was involved seemed to be his main reason for sadness dips, and the source of his known spells of depression.

The preface of this book is where the fictionalised version of Peter was quoted to say:

Come away, come away!

'...that strange and terrible summer...' [3]

This is a line that many mistake to have been actually said from Peter in later years, and use it to build a case against Barrie and his relationship with the Llewelyn Davies boys, but it was never actually spoken by the real Peter, only said by a four-year-old version of Peter in a story.

Whilst Barrie kept one copy of this book for himself, the other was gifted to Arthur Llewelyn Davies, a novel keepsake for the father of such delightful boys. However, Arthur very quickly (and suspiciously conveniently) lost his copy by leaving it on a train, which may very well reflect his true feelings on the writer and his involvement with his family. Peter remarked in later years that this was 'doubtless his own way of commenting on the whole fantastic affair.' [4]

At least Barrie still had the boys for the summer; no school to interrupt and no city engagements with young friends to distract them.

But the fun was always going to come to an end; come September, the boys were due back to school and Barrie was met with an unexpected trip to Scotland when more death came to interject his life. His sister, Isabella, had passed away, though she was only two years older than himself. He travelled to attend her funeral.

And then Porthos, his most faithful companion, came to the end of his life, and marked the end of an era not only for Barrie and the stories involving him but also the beginning of the end of his marriage. The loyal and loving dog had been keeping the pair preoccupied and tied together with the most fragile thread, but with the house now empty of his joyful presence, the two became more and more aware of their issues. Mary Ansell wrote of the solemn occasion:

> *'When it became impossible to have him any longer about the house, he was sent to that humane institution, the Dogs' Home at Battersea, and in the lethal chamber he was put peacefully to sleep. Buried with him were... those first seven years of my married life.'* [5]

Come 1902, *The Little White Bird* was finally ready for publication and released to the eager hands of the public.

The Dark Side of Peter Pan

Its reception was generally very positive; a book critic from *The Times* wrote:

> '*The book is all Barrie-ness; whimsical, sentimental, profound, ridiculous Barrie-ness; utterly impossible, yet absolutely real, a fairy tower built on the eternal truth... this is one of the best things that Mr Barrie has written. From beginning to end it is a fantasy, of fairies, birds, old bachelors... pretty young wives and their children – but especially their children. If a book exists which contains more knowledge and more love of children, we do not know it... Mr Barrie has given us the best of himself, and we can think of no higher praise.*'

Additionally, many people found his clear understanding of children rather endearing, especially when he doted on so many children and not just the boys that inspired his stories. Dolly (family friend of the Llewelyn Davies') wrote of him in her diary:

> '*...his devotion & genius-like understanding of children is beautiful & touching beyond words – as he has none himself.*'[6]

In fact, many mothers would rush at him when catching sight of the famous writer in Kensington Gardens with the hopes that their own children would bask in the glow of his paternal affections. Pushing them to be friendly with the man, however, only irritated him; refusing to let children be exploited for recognition is a bare minimum quality but still admirable for a person living in that world.

And Barrie wasn't the only one reaping the attention from the book's fame; since it was apparent that David's character in *The Little White Bird* was based on the young George, he attained a lot of attention at his school – Wilkinson's – and was also teased a little for his belief in fairies. Although he was recorded to not be bothered by the taunting, it's easy to imagine that such a young child being thrown into the spotlight and mocked for his involvement would eventually affect him in the years to come.

In more recent times – and in light of multiple terrible revelations concerning celebrities previously loved by the public – a new eye has been cast over some of the text in *The Little White Bird*. Barrie's noted thoughts and behaviours are extremely delicate to approach in terms of how inappropriate they've been deemed, since it is agreeably questionable. The following extract, for example, is a key instance where eyebrows have been raised:

> '...David watched my preparations with distasteful levity, but anon made a noble amend by abruptly offering me his foot as if he had no longer use for it, and I knew by intuition that he expected me to take off his boots. I took them off with all the coolness of an old hand, and then I placed him on my knee and removed his blouse. This was a delightful experience, but I think I remained wonderfully calm until I came somewhat too suddenly to his little braces, which agitated me profoundly.
> 'I cannot proceed in public with the disrobing of David.'[7]

This passage already raises some concern, and a few paragraphs later:

> ' "Why David," said I, sitting up, "do you want to come into my bed?"
> ' "Mother said I wasn't to want it unless you wanted it first," he squeaked.'
> ' "It is what I have been wanting all the time," said I, and then without much more ado the little white figure rose and flung itself at me. For the rest of the night he lay on me and across me, and sometimes his feet were at the bottom of the bed and sometimes on the pillow, but he always retained possession of my finger, and occasionally he woke me to say that he was sleeping with me.'[8]

Despite many having thrown out the words 'paedophilic' and 'perverted' upon reading this for the first time in the modern era, a different view must be thrown in for consideration. These passages represent Barrie's yearnings for being a father and taking joy in the simple things that parents do not always take note of. Consider, rather than him feeling alarmed at an attraction to a little boy, the over-excitement of a man who longs for a son. Evidence for this is supported in the later line:

> *'Of how I had stood by the open door listening to his sweet breathing, had stood so long that I forgot his name and called him Timothy.'*[9]

Timothy, of course, being the son he wished for but would never have.

Barrie was merely taking delight in some of the simple acts of parenting, ones that he would not usually be a part of for other people's children. He knew that he would never have a son of his own because that would involve a sexual relationship with his wife, something that he probably wasn't entirely capable of due to a speculated asexuality, in which a term had not been coined yet. The theory of his asexuality being the source of all this is a very new and modern theory, but entirely possible. Sexuality is a topic that many consider 'newly invented', but in previous decades and even centuries, it was simply deemed inappropriate and unaccepted. Not being understood would mean that those being anything other than heterosexual would live a life of secrecy, and Barrie would've been no different. Who could he have talked to about his feelings, or lack of feelings? How would he blatantly record them without the fear that their discovery would have him scorned?

The famous writer was so young at heart that he even recorded how he bought himself toys but let on that they were for his imaginary son:

> *'The dame in the temple of toys which we frequent thinks I want them for a little boy and calls him 'the precious' and 'the lamb', the while Porthos is standing gravely at my side.'*[10]

He never corrected the woman behind the counter when she referred to the imaginary boy, most likely from embarrassment.

As the success of *The Little White Bird* continued and sales were maintained, Barrie and his wife made the move from Gloucester Road to a small Regency house in Bayswater Road, Leinster Corner, which overlooked the north of Kensington Gardens. Mary was once again left with the distraction of renovating and organising the house, just as she had been previously set the task with Black Lake Cottage. Barrie got on with entertaining the Llewelyn Davies boys with continued stories and working on a few new projects.

Come away, come away!

The distractions from his marriage were only replaced with yet another grievance for him, however, with the death of Barrie's father. News from Kirriemuir reached London that David Barrie Sr. had died after being knocked down by a horse and cart – he was 87. Once again, the Barrie's travelled up through Scotland and back to his hometown to attend the funeral, before inviting the family to stay at Black Lake Cottage as a kind gesture in light of their combined grief.

For Barrie, it only made the atmosphere depressing; he was only too glad to welcome the Llewelyn Davies family for a summer stay as soon as his own family had departed. This improved his mood greatly – a great escape from another death he'd faced – and it was another summer filled with games on the lake and sparks of inspiration for his writing. A new idea for a play was beginning to take shape, in which the character of Peter would make his next, and most famous, appearance.

To celebrate the success of *The Little White Bird*, Barrie took Sylvia away to Paris, a gesture that Arthur was probably exasperated by. In a letter to his father, John Llewelyn Davies, the vicar of Kirby Lonsdale at the time, he wrote:

> *'It is just possible that Sylvia may be induced to come too, but that is not likely... Sylvia is at present on a trip to Paris with her friends the Barries...'*[11]

Arthur's feelings towards Barrie at this time seem to be heavily suggested by the use of 'her friends' rather than 'our friends' – he didn't seem to hold the man in high regard at all, whether or not he felt any real threat from him at all. What Barrie's own wife thought isn't recorded at all, though she must've thrown some concern about what this gesture from Barrie to Sylvia may look like to others.

When 1903 dawned, Mary decided on getting another dog, this time a black and white Newfoundland called Luath. Luath was ultimately the end visual representation for Nana in *Peter Pan* due to his affection for children. He seemed to be another receptacle for a child that Barrie could not have, as Mary came to write of him:

> *'Luath's proper place was in the nursery. How happy he would have been if there had been one, full of gloriously noisy children!'*[12]

It is evident that Mary still seemed to long for a child, demonstrated through her need to mother *something* she could call her own. Luath's love for children – another aspect of Nana's character – may have caused her some pain to see, since it was as if even Luath longed for the child Mary would never have. That, and he was Barrie's loyal companion, as he walked Kensington Gardens with a dog by his side again.

The summer came around and Sylvia was pregnant with her fifth child. She and her family spent another holiday with Barrie at Black Lake Cottage, and Michael was now big enough to take on more capable roles in the games played with Barrie and his brothers down at the lake, much to Barrie's delight.

Spending so much time with a man that wasn't at all family must've led to speculation about the kind of involvement that he had with them, but Barrie was just relishing in caring for a family that he'd adopted to be his own. Hosting them at his summer home as often as he did – much more often than his own family by blood – just showed that he was dedicated to them in a completely selfless manner. All he wanted was time with the boys, time that was going too fast for him. Confessing to the boys in his Dedication to *Peter Pan* years later, he talked about Peter Pan not being his own creation at all, giving them all the credit:

> *'You had played it until you tired of it, and tossed it in the air and gored it and left it derelict in the mud and went on your way singing other songs; and then I stole back and sewed some of the gory fragments together with a pen-nib. That is what must have happened, but I cannot remember doing it.'* [13]

In November of 1903, Sylvia gave birth to her fifth son, named Nicholas, quickly known only as Nico. It seemed to perfectly mark the occasion of Barrie beginning work on his new play the day before, a play about The Boy Who Wouldn't Grow Up. His initial draft was all handwritten and is luckily still in existence, stored in the Library of Indiana University.

Sylvia and Arthur, now with five boys, concluded that they were too large a family for their house in Kensington Park Gardens, and Arthur had a wish to move out of London and to a house in the country. Whether this was a traditional dream to give his children more room and space to raise them or a way to put some space between them and Barrie, there's no proof.

Come away, come away!

The Llewelyn Davies family made the move to Egerton House on Berkhamstead High Street as a result, and it was to everyone's convenience: it was spacious, close to the station for Arthur's London commute, and it was close to a school for the boys.

It was also twenty-five miles from Mr Barrie's house.

At least he had his new play; he finished writing it on 1st March 1904, referring to it at this point as *Peter and Wendy*.

Unlike all his previously written plays, this one was going to be extremely high-budget and full of extravagancies. Huge sets, multiple characters of varying species and cast members needing to fly across the stage were all red flags for any producer, especially considering that the idea of making people look as if they were flying was relatively new to the theatre. When Barrie showed it to Beerbohm Tree – an actor-manager associated with His Majesty's Theatre – he claimed that 'Barrie must be mad'. He even went so far as to write to Charles Frohman before Barrie had the chance to present *Peter and Wendy* to him, to 'warn' him that Barrie had 'gone out of his mind'.

However, when Frohman actually came to read what Barrie was now referring to as *The Great White Father* in April 1904, he fell in love with the play. He wanted it to be at the West End by Christmas of that year, along with a US run set for the following year that would star Maude Adams as Peter. His only qualm was that the title be changed, to which Barrie approved, and it was agreed upon as *Peter Pan*.[14]

Writing and revising the script ready for casting was the best distraction for Barrie too, since the Llewelyn Davies family did not holiday at all at Black Lake Cottage that year. Instead, they spent the summer settling into their new home at Egerton House.

By the time rehearsals for *Peter Pan* started in October 1904, Nina Boucicault had been cast as the first ever Peter, whilst Hilda Trevelyan was cast to play Wendy. The tradition of having a woman play the young Peter was to give the best appearance of passing for a young boy since hiring an actual young boy wasn't possible; being small with a high voice were the basic requirements to convince the audience.

Barrie set the roles of Mr Darling and Captain Hook to be played by one actor, which under literary analysis, was to reflect on how Wendy is a little afraid of her father, who tells her that she must grow up. Because of his treatment of Nana in the opening act, Wendy loses respect for Mr Darling and, in a way, Hook is the manifestation of this fear and loss of respect and all the bad that can come of it. On the other hand, Wendy is consistently fascinated by Hook and his charm throughout the story, which leads to her consideration of letting go of her childhood, and submitting to growing up when she tells her brothers that they must return home to their parents.

Barrie offered this twin role to Sylvia's brother and the actor, Gerald du Maurier, who accepted the part. Gerald's daughter, Daphne du Maurier, wrote of her father as Captain Hook in *Gerald: A Portrait*:[15]

> '*Gerald* was *Hook*; he was no dummy dressed from Simmons' in a Clarkson wig, ranting and roaring about the stage, a grotesque figure whom the modern child finds a little comic. He was a tragic and rather ghastly creation who knew no peace, and whose soul was in torment; a dark shadow; a sinister dream; a bogey of fear who lives perpetually in the grey recesses of every small boy's mind. All boys had their Hooks, as Barrie knew; he was the phantom who came by night and stole his way into their murky dreams... Gerald made him alive.'

The rest of the cast consisted of the following:

- Joan Burnett (Tootles)
- Christine Silver (Nibs)
- A.W. Baskcomb (Slightly)
- Alice DuBarry (Curly)
- Pauline Chase (1st twin)
- Phyllis Beadon (2nd twin)
- George Hersee (John)
- Dorothea Baird (Mrs Darling)
- Arthur Lupino (Nana)
- Winifred Geoghegan (Michael)
- George Shelton (Smee)
- Sidney Harcourt (Gentleman Starkey)
- Charles Trevor (Cookson)
- Frederick Annerley (Cecco)
- Hubert Willis (Mullins)

Come away, come away!

- James English (Jukes)
- John Kelt (Noodler)
- Philip Darwin (Great Big Little Panther)
- Miriam Nesbitt (Tiger Lily)
- Ela Q. May (Liza)
- First Pirate (Gerald Malvern)
- Second Pirate (J. Grahame)
- Black Pirate (S. Spencer)
- Crocodile (A. Ganker & C. Lawton)
- Ostrich (G. Henson)
- Tinker Bell was represented on stage by a darting light.

When Hilda Trevelyan (playing Wendy) arrived to her first rehearsal, she was met with quite an alarming request: she was informed that she would need to have her life insured for the flying sequences.

The flying systems – harnesses and wires – were all completely produced anew for the play so that they weren't so visible and bulky on the actors and could be removed quickly so they needn't stay on for an entire scene. George Kirby, of Kirby's Flying Ballet Company, was personally anointed by Barrie to make this more effective system, which he did with the invention of a new harness.

Barrie spent the rehearsals pining for the five Llewelyn Davies boys, and wrote to Peter on 3rd November:

> *'Sometimes when I am walking in the Gardens with Luath I see a vision and I cry, Hurray, there's Peter, and then Luath barks joyously and we run to the vision and then it turns out to be not Peter but just another boy, and then I cry like a water cart and Luath hangs his sorrowful tail... how I wish you were here, and then it would be London again.'*[16]

There's no doubt that Barrie's missing them was because they were not getting to see their story come to life as he was. That, and they were his greatest friends, his escape from adulthood and the polite society he was now having to endeavor in with working on the play.

To further mimic the contribution of George, Jack, Peter and Michael, Sylvia had supplied a basketful of the boys' clothes to be copied and remade for the Darling children; Barrie's inclusion of the boys seemed to have no end. And when Sylvia brought them to the rehearsals in early December, Barrie escorted them around as if they were royalty, introducing them to others as 'the real authors of the play' and holding up the entire schedule for them to try out flying around the stage. Anxieties ran high with cast and crew because of the delays, which would later come to affect the author too.

In the run up to the opening night of the play – which was originally set for 22nd December – so many things seemed to go wrong that the date had to be pushed back. To begin with, a mechanical lift collapsed, cutting down a lot of the scenery in the process. Some of the scenery also remained unfinished, fine as it was in detail, as well as mechanical gear needed for the effects not having been installed yet.

Finally, on 27th December 1904, *Peter Pan*, or *The Boy Who Wouldn't Grow Up*, opened for the first time on stage at the Duke of York's Theatre in London. An anxious Barrie waited on the sidelines, watching the audience for their reaction intently. It was a play that the high society audience were not going to expect from someone so well-established and, should it fail, the author's reputation could've been forever ruined.

Chapter 6

"Do you know," Peter asked, "why swallows build in the eaves of houses? It is to listen to the stories" 1904–1905

When the curtain rose on *Peter Pan*, showing the Darling nursery, the audience at first were struck into silence: it was absolutely nothing like what they were expecting from the esteemed playwright. But the story had them captivated right from the start; the mysterious flying boy that talked of a magical island where fairies and mermaids and pirates dwelled was a new concept seen on stage for the audience. They remained engaged and intrigued as the play went from a London nursery to a mermaid lagoon, from a pirate ship to an underground home. They watched in awe as the actors flew across the stage and the elaborate sets came to life before them.

When the crucial scene of Tinker Bell's demise arrived, it was the moment of truth for Barrie; it was a gamble whether the adult audience would participate. In preparation for the worst-case scenario, Barrie had arranged for the orchestra to clap in place of the audience, should they not take to the charming proposal.

> '***PETER*** *Do you believe in fairies? Say quick that you believe!*
> *If you believe, clap your hands!*'[1]

When asked for their belief in fairies, the response was a moving surprise of loud clapping and cheers from the entire theatre audience, which sent many of the cast and crew members into emotional tears.

It was in this moment that J.M. Barrie had taken theatre and entered it into a new age.

The end of the performance was a rippling effect of praise and applause, and Barrie himself was met with equal admiration.

The Daily Telegraph published their review soon after:

> *'...so touching that it brought the audience to the writer's feet and held them captive there.'*

And the *Saturday Review* said:

> *'Here, at last, we see [Barrie's] talent in its full maturity; for here he has stripped off from himself the last flimsy remnants of a pretense to maturity...*

The play was a success for so many reasons amongst an Edwardian audience. Ultimately, the idea was for the grown-ups watching it to regain their sense of childhood, and with some of the mature dialogue thrown in amongst the child-like themes, it appealed to them:

> *'Oh dear, I am sure I sometimes think that spinsters are to be envied.'* [2]

The flying sequences were magical to watch, the characters delightful, and the pinnacle of this engagement was involving the audience at the climax of the play.

The play also seemed to anticipate its own potential criticisms, as one stage direction provided a metaphor for those that would turn their nose up at the play:

> *'You can't see Peter if you are old.'* [3]

Furthermore, if anyone didn't see the joy of *Peter Pan*, it was because they'd completely lost touch with their inner child.

The most anticipated guests were finally to see the play after spending Christmas at Berkhamstead; George, Jack, Peter and Michael Llewelyn Davies were recorded to have thoroughly enjoyed the play that their Uncle Jimmy wrote, as well as the recognition that they were considered as the co-writers as well.

"Do you know," Peter asked, "why swallows build in the eaves of houses?

But for Barrie, the huge success of his new play seemed to be hitting a dull wall: *Peter Pan* was his greatest joy, but the popularity of it in the hands of the public took the joy from him. In his Dedication to the boys in 1928, Barrie wrote:

> '...Peter is as far away in the woods as that laughter of yours in which he came into being long before he was caught and written down... There is Peter still, but to me he lies sunk in that gay Black Lake. '[4]

It was almost as if the play had served its true purpose to him well before it was put on stage, in the summer days when Barrie's adventures with the boys seemed like they would go on forever. At the end of *Peter and Wendy*, Peter faces a similar situation when watching on in the final scene in the Darling nursery, his adventures with Wendy, John, Michael, and the Lost Boys behind him:

> '[Peter] had had ecstasies innumerable that other children can never know; but he was looking through the window at the one joy from which he must be forever barred. '[5]

He had written the play to stay locked in those summer memories for a little longer, as he wrote in *A Window in Thrums*:

> '...it is sweeter to hold on to what has been than to think of what may be. '[6]

Barrie had poured his whole self into the story, and for those 'in the know' it wasn't difficult to note that many of Hook's traits were autobiographical to Barrie. His days playing Captain Swarthy at Black Lake Cottage had helped develop Hook's character, and he morphed himself into the pirate as well. Hook is described as 'a dark and sinister man' with 'a touch of the feminine'. He was also left-handed, just as the writer was. One, particular description for Hook stands out amongst them all, however:

> 'He is never more sinister than when he is most polite, and the elegance of his diction, the distinction of his demeanor, show

> *him one of a different class from his crew, a solitary among uncultured companions.'*[7]

Could this have been how Barrie saw himself? To be sure he struggled in social situations amongst members of high society, and he found other adults not nearly as interesting in conversation as their children, but he knew his way of thinking was on a completely different level to those around him.

Meanwhile, Peter's character sported all of Barrie's incapable traits.

Whilst Wendy proves undoubtedly that she loves Peter in a romantic way, Peter doesn't grasp it at all. As Wendy is still only a child, her understanding of romantic love is what she would've seen in other couples, including her parents, just as other children would. Peter, however, makes it clear that he sees all girls as mothers. Everything – including playing at mother and father with Wendy – is through pretend with him.

> '**WENDY** *What is wrong, Peter?*
>
> **PETER** *(scared) It is only pretend, isn't it, that I am their father?*
>
> **WENDY** *(drooping) Oh, yes.*
>
> *(His sigh of relief is without consideration for her feelings)*
>
> *But they are ours, Peter, yours and mine.*
>
> **PETER** *(determined to get at facts, the only things that puzzle him) But not really?*
>
> **WENDY** *Not if you don't wish it.*
>
> **PETER** *I don't.*
>
> **WENDY** *(knowing she ought not to probe but driven to it by something within) What are your exact feelings for me, Peter?*
>
> **PETER** *(in the class-room) Those of a devoted son, Wendy.*
>
> **WENDY** *(turning away) I thought so.'*[8]

It is very similar to Barrie's games with Mary Ansell – the flirting, the courting, and the skirting around any kind of commitment to her. It was only when the outward social pressure of expecting a marriage between

"Do you know," Peter asked, "why swallows build in the eaves of houses?

them pushed him to propose. Having never really wanted to enter into a serious union and only taking pleasure in the fun of the chase, it explains why he suddenly grew so cold towards her after they finally married.

For Mary, it must've been even more difficult to see Mrs Darling floating across the stage, knowing who the model for her had clearly been.

> '*She is the loveliest lady in Bloomsbury, with a sweet mocking mouth...*'[9]

To Barrie, Sylvia was the ultimate mother, the epitome of maternal love and care. Who better to play the only actual mother in the play? Moreover, his fascination with and appreciation of mothers was the frequent topic of conversation among the characters.

> '***TOOTLES*** *I am awfully anxious about Cinderella. You see, not knowing anything about my own mother I am fond of thinking she was rather like Cinderella.*
> *(This is received with derision)*
>
> ***NIBS*** *All I remember about my mother is that she often said to father, 'Oh, how I wish I had a cheque book of my own.' I don't know what a cheque book is, but I should just love to give my mother one.*
>
> ***SLIGHTLY*** *(as usual) My mother was fonder of me than your mothers were of you. (Uproar) Oh yes, she was.*
>
> ...
>
> ***TOOTLES*** *When ladies used to come to me in dreams I said 'Pretty mother'...*'[10]

The following year in May of 1905, Charles Frohman announced advanced bookings for *Peter Pan*'s re-opening in the December. Its success and demand for a return from the public pretty much guaranteed an equal success for its second year running, and Frohman only heightened the anticipation by selling tickets as early as he did.

In response, Barrie had Sylvia and Michael to stay at Black Lake Cottage for a couple of weeks in June to reignite inspiration and revise the script.

From reports in the first run, he had to add in that you could only fly if you had happy thoughts *and* fairy dust, in order to stop children from harming themselves by jumping from high places in their attempts to fly away.

As was the usual old routine: Barrie took Michael down to the lake for games and stories. It was on one of these adventures that Michael developed an unnatural terror of water, and no one was able to extract from him what exactly happened there to cause it, not even his mother. Afterwards, he was never able to swim more than twenty yards and despite Barrie's attempts to help him, the lessons from the person Barrie hired over a three-week period were to no avail.

Michael's fear also induced nightmares that would wake him frequently; Daphne du Maurier recalled to author Andrew Birkin from her Nanny's memory that Michael would wake in the middle of the night and 'see strange people and things coming in through the window.'[11] It was as if Michael believed that Peter Pan was a completely real being, who was out there frolicking among the stars.

Barrie's involvement of the boys appeared to be going too far, all for the sake of inspiration for his Peter Pan stories. However, he seemed to genuinely feel that he owed his success to the Llewelyn Davies children, that they really were the true authors of his tales from Neverland. Their involvement was absolutely vital to him.

And he wasn't very good at hiding his clear tendency for favourites among them, either. It was obvious to everyone close to him who had the spotlight for his inspiration; Nico wrote in 1975:

> *'...we all knew that George and Michael were The Ones – George because he had started it all, and Michael... because he was the cleverest of us, the most original, the potential genius.'*[12]

It was never outright stated by Barrie that George and Michael were his gems, but the fact that the other boys felt it means that it was probably common but unspoken knowledge in the family. It only makes their future filled with a tragic irony, and the speculation it would lead to in later years is understandable, but misread.

"Do you know," Peter asked, "why swallows build in the eaves of houses?

Peter Pan opened in the US on November 6th 1905, with Maude Adams starring as the title role of Peter. The American audience received it with just as much enthusiasm, if not more, and it was clear to Frohman that the international success of the play held high hopes for the future.

Mark Twain's unofficial review of the play was written in a letter he sent to Maude Adams after the opening performance, where amongst his praise of her acting, he described the play as:

> *'...a great and refining and uplifting benefaction to this sordid and money-mad age.'*

In light of the predicted success in the US, Charles Frohman had Maude Adams tour the entire States in not just the large city theatres, but also theatres situated in smaller towns. The story of The Boy Who Wouldn't Grow Up was reaching every corner, causing joy for both adults and children.

The international hit throughout all of its audiences made Frohman more than happy, but for Barrie the fame was lost on him.

In 1906 alone, James Barrie made £44,000, approximately £3.7 million in 2021 money according to inflation. By this time, he was able to donate to dozens of charities as well as live more than just comfortably with his wife and dog. With a property in London, another in the countryside, as well as frequent trips abroad, by today's standards that was a wealthy way of life. And yet the air of melancholy swirled around Barrie. Perhaps it's because within all the delightfulness and fun of the story, people were missing the point of Peter's true character.

Barrie's Peter was lost on its endless audiences. The original Peter that Barrie had written as a raw depiction of an adult's inability to grow up was an exposure unto himself, and he'd released it into the world bravely, only to not be seen. Peter's character, upon closer inspection, appears almost sociopathic, and is a bit of an antihero. For example, he is completely unsympathetic, particularly in the moment when Wendy is 'killed' after being shot down by one of the Lost Boys.

> *'He is not so much pained as puzzled.'*[13]

He has witnessed a horror, and yet isn't horrified. It should be remembered that Peter is actually quite dangerous; it's told that he 'thins out' the Lost

Boys if they are growing too old – in other words, execution. He is not as innocent as many would like to continue to believe.

> *'(How he would like to rip those stories out of her; he is dangerous now.)'*[14]

In fact, many forget that Peter Pan started as some kind of spirit that walked with children part of the way to the afterlife so that they wouldn't be so scared as they died, and in the future adaptation of his story it's heavily implied that he isn't an actual child. He is, as Old Soloman in *The Little White Bird* called him, a 'betwixt-and-between'.

> *'(with a drum beating in his breast as if he were a real boy at last)'*[15]

Even at the end of the play, Wendy says of him:

> *'...he would think all the past was yesterday...'*[16]

Just as a God or an entity who lives forever might. Peter is not a real boy, only represents the spirit of a boy, the recklessness and playfulness.

> *'It has something to do with the riddle of his being.'*[17]

Peter carries on in Neverland forgetting every day as soon as it ends, believing honestly: 'I just want always to be a little boy and to have fun.', though '...it is only his greatest pretend.'[18]

In the 1904 rehearsal script, Peter says to Mrs Darling:

> *'But I'll be good to the dead babies, I shall come and sing gaily to them when the bell tolls; and then they won't be frightened. I shall dance by their graves and they will clap their hands to me...'*[19]

He truly speaks with the understanding of a God, despite showing no understanding of many other mature things like romantic love. In another stage direction:

"Do you know," Peter asked, "why swallows build in the eaves of houses?

'*...and in his dreams he is always in pursuit of a boy who was never here, nor anywhere: the only boy who could beat him.* '[20]

This could be the boy Peter could've become if he hadn't flown from the nursery to live among the fairies, before he became the betwixt-and-between. A boy who would've loved a girl romantically, a boy who would've grown up to be a man and had children of his own, a boy who *would've* lived, to see the awfully big adventure of simply living – but evidently, could not. And ultimately, this is how Barrie felt trapped; this is how he saw himself.

It would've been an adventure for Barrie to have all those things but in his mind, he forever remained young and 'an innocent'. Just like his signature character, he couldn't grow up, either.

With countless runs of *Peter Pan* still going in theatres today, many renditions relying on comedy for the sake of creating entertaining pantomimes, it can't be helped to note that Barrie's Peter is no longer portrayed faithfully. The Peter we see now was probably tainted by Disney's version, with all the gory details removed and only the magical elements highlighted. It set the way for future versions, where adaptations like *Hook* (1991) missed the point of Peter's being, suggesting that he would be capable of leaving the Neverland and feeling romantic love towards someone.

To come across an accurate representation of Barrie's Peter now is rare, and a treasure, especially when you are aware of the history and the story behind the boy who wouldn't – or rather, couldn't – grow up.

Chapter 7

So the older ones have become glassy-eyed and seldom speak... but the little ones still wonder
1905–1907

As Barrie's fame continued to climb, the Llewelyn Davies family were settling into life in the country. Their new home at Egerton House was a great fit for them, as their family friend Dolly wrote of in her diary:

> '...nothing could be more perfect than the inside, especially for so large a family. There are huge nurseries & a schoolroom with mullioned windows which occupy the whole length of the rooms... all so charmingly done as only Sylvia can do things,,, Sylvia, who is as dear as ever she was. I like to see her at luncheon at the head of her long table in the beautiful Hall with its huge windows & great 16th century chimney piece – serving food to 4 beautiful boys who all have perfect manners & are most agreeable companions, especially George. Arthur came down in the evening, looking handsome and severe.'[1]

There was a nearby school for the boys, and Arthur now had the space to play with and spend more time with his sons, who he was incredibly gentle with despite the norm of the time; the general understanding was that harsh fathers brought up strong boys to grow into 'proper' men. Dolly wrote of Arthur:

> 'He was so tender and gentle with children that I never met one who feared him, in spite of his rather severe though wonderful looks.'[2]

So the older ones have become glassy-eyed and seldom speak…

All in all, the whole family were benefitting from the move away from the big city, and despite the new distance from their writer friend, Barrie still made frequent visits to the family; he still took Sylvia away on frequent trips to Paris and Dives in Normandy with at least one or more of the boys in tow. His presence in their lives remained a constant, as Barrie did not let the distance part him from his boys.

The new life and its joys were short-lived, however.

It was in May of 1906 that Arthur uncovered a physical ailment in a letter to his sister Margaret:

> *'I had been hoping to manage a visit to Kirkby with Michael this Whitsuntide, to fit in with Sylvia's outing, but I am doomed to spend Whitsuntide less agreeably – in lying up for a small operation. I have a slight swelling in the side of the face, which is beyond the dentist's skill, and on his advice I consulted an expert in cheek and jaw. He is going to perform on Friday, and I shall stay at a nursing place till the following Tuesday. Probably the cause of the trouble is the root of an old dead tooth, possibly a minute fragment of a tooth long ago pulled out… I expect to be more or less recovered after a week.'*[3]

The operation initially appeared to be a success, and not of major concern in terms of the prospect of Arthur's health. Sylvia wrote to Margaret on 1st June to let her know that Arthur was doing well and she hoped to have him home soon, but on 2nd June, Arthur wrote:

> *'Dearest Margaret,*
> *I am sorry to say that I have had bad news. The swelling in my face turns out on investigation not to be an abscess, as was hoped, but a growth. It is of a very serious kind, called sarcoma, and requires a grave operation… I am afraid it means removing half the upper jaw and palate… Poor Sylvia! I have told her everything except the name of the disease and the details of the operation. She is brave and infinitely kind and dear. After the operation I shall be incapacitated for about 6 weeks, and unable to speak properly for 3 or 4 months – and*

there will always be an impediment in my speech. I think of our future and the boys.

We shall be very glad if you will come up on Monday and help us through this trying time... My 43 years, and especially the last 14, leaves me no ground of complaint as to my life. But this needs fortitude. We both try our best.

My love to Father.

Your affect. brother,
A.Ll.D.[4]

In other words, it was a tumour that the doctors had found, and it was cancerous.

As soon as Barrie heard of Arthur's illness, he abandoned all other responsibility and cancelled all engagements in order to visit the family and lay his claim to foot the bill for all potential medical fees. He made it clear that he would make sure Arthur had the best treatment available at the time, submitting himself to the family as a ready servant for anything further they might possibly need. Although some may perceive this behaviour as quite intense or desperate, Barrie saw it as nothing more than being a dedicated friend to the people he saw not only as his dearest friends, but as family.

In later years, Peter wrote of this time:

'J.M.B. stepped in to play the leading part; and played it in the grand manner... I can sympathise in a way with the point of view that it was the last straw for Arthur that he should have had to accept charity from the strange little genius who had become such an increasing irritation to him in recent years. But on the whole I disagree. We don't really know how deep the irritation went; and even if it went deep, I am convinced that the kindness and devotion of which J.M.B. gave such overwhelming proof from now on, far more than outweighed all that, and that the money and promise of future financial responsibility he was so ready with – and with what charm and tact he must have overcome any resistance! – were an incalculable comfort to the doomed Arthur as well as to Sylvia in her anguish.'[5]

So the older ones have become glassy-eyed and seldom speak…

The general feeling here indicates that Peter thought his father had really despised Barrie but was humbled by his illness; even if Arthur had held dislike for the man in the past, he appeared genuinely warmed by his generosity not only in a financial sense, but in the way he would tend to Arthur at his bedside.

> *'Barrie has been wonderful to us – we look on him as a brother.'*[6]

Arthur's biggest operation took place on 8th June. Part of his jaw and cheekbone were removed in an attempt to eradicate the cancer. When Barrie reached his bedside to be there for when he woke, Arthur's face was almost entirely bandaged. Barrie read him the newspaper through the night, holding his hand and when he was strong enough, encouraging him to 'talk' through writing.

Completely unable to speak, Arthur communicated through writing notes, many of which are still preserved. One of them was:

> *Among the things I think about*
> *Michael going to school*
> *Porthgwarra and S's blue dress*
> *Burpha, garden*
> *Kirkby view across valley*
> *Jack bathing*
> *Peter answering chaff*
> *Nicholas in the garden*
> *George always*[7]

Arthur's thoughts continued to revolve around his family, his children being the centre of his world. Loving them as dearly as he did is adamantly clear, as he was not anxious to show his feelings towards them unlike most fathers of the era. Despite Arthur's operation being a general success at this point, it was as if his brush with death only made him all the more fond of his boys and keen to be active in their lives.

When Arthur's bandages came off a week later, Sylvia was devastated:

> *'They've spoilt my darling's face.'*[8]

With much of his face missing, it must've been quite a shock to her, though she was still reported to be extremely attentive to him in his care and did her best not to let on to him of her distress.

Barrie also remained at his side, like a shadow to its owner. Arthur wrote to Peter that evening:

> *'Don't you think Mr Barrie is a very good friend to all of us?'*[9]

As Arthur recuperated in a private house away from his still-young children, his sister Margaret resided at Egerton House to help take care of the boys, who were constantly warned and made aware of their father's new appearance to get them used to the idea. It was in everyone's best interests that they not act too shocked.

Finally, Arthur was in a good enough place to return home, and Sylvia was proud of her sons for their reception of him:

> *'The little boys are really wonderfully good, and so far... all is well.'*[10]

On July 5th, Arthur was measured for an artificial jaw to be fitted, most likely to assist in a practical sense. Peter later said of it:

> *'I am not sure that the ghastly plate, or artificial jaw, isn't the most dreadful element in the whole sad story. It must have been a nightmare, and so much seemed to depend on it, and it so soon became impossible to wear...'*[11]

The jaw was apparently not a positive addition.

All the while, Barrie's career had been placed on hold. Nothing came above the priority of caring for the Llewelyn Davies family, and it was no bother to the playwright if all his projects came to a standstill. His devotion to the boys and their parents took precedence above all else, and whilst holidaying at Cudlow House in Rustington during the summer of 1906, it can't help being noted that Arthur was now referring to Barrie as 'Jimmy' rather than just 'Sylvia's friend'.

> So the older ones have become glassy-eyed and seldom speak...
>
> *'...the boys play endless cricket and lawn tennis in the garden. Just now we have an invasion by some friend of Jimmy's...'*[12]

Arthur was perhaps starting to miss his copy of *The Boy Castaways*, as he requested the other and only copy for his stay in hospital. The photographs of his sons brought him great comfort when he was unable to see them in person.

This was also the summer where some of the most famous photographs of Michael were taken – dressed as Peter Pan with Barrie playing the role of Captain Hook. These photos alone showcase just how much Barrie adored Michael, and how close a bond the pair had. If anything untoward or inappropriate had occurred between them, discomfort would probably be more plain on Michael's face, but he shows no such distress.

When Dolly Ponsonby went to visit them all at their retreat in Rustington, she praised Barrie's devotion to the family, including the particular care he took of Arthur in his recovery:

> *'Mr Barrie is always with him, a nurse to the children & an extraordinary, tactful & helpful companion to Sylvia and Arthur – though his moods like those of most genius types appear to me a little trying.'*[13]

These 'trying' moods were Barrie's bouts of silence which many of the extroverted characters of society would've found rude or odd. Being such an introvert made Barrie appear unapproachable even when he was only offering help and kindness.

It was clear that he was around to assist with anything he could, so much was he devoted to Sylvia and in turn her own devotion of Arthur. Perhaps his care was what humbled Arthur to consider him as a friend as well, seeing that not only was he not at all a threat to his marriage, but also completely and innocently dedicated to his wife and sons. The family friend was not trying to replace Arthur in any way, only wanting to be a part of the family by extension.

The stay at Rustington had been needed for everyone to adjust to the new life they faced after the trauma of Arthur's surgery. With five young boys that were still to be put through school, it would've been a very concerning time for everyone, and it was initially unknown just how well Arthur would take to things after. When the family and playwright returned home, Arthur wrote to Barrie:

> *Dear Jimmy,*
> *You have done wonderful things for us since the beginning of June – most, of course, during June and also in the last week – but at Rustington also you made all the difference to the success and pleasantness of the holiday. We all hope to see you soon and often.*
>
> *Yours*
> *A.Ll.D.*[14]

It seemed as if the worst was over at least, and all that was left to do was adapt and come up with a new normal. However, when Arthur visited his specialist only two days after the return home, he was informed that the tumour had spread, and that another operation couldn't be done to remove it.

On 18th September, Arthur wrote to his sister Margaret:

> *'I asked how far off the end would be, but he could not say – perhaps 6 months or a year… Of course what I care about now is to give [Sylvia] all the support I can, and also, if the worst comes, to leave her with memories of the remaining time which will afterwards be a comfort rather than an unhappiness. I myself have consolations and even occasions of poignant happiness such as could not come to any man who had no wife and children. My burden is far less heavy than Sylvia's.'*[15]

Arthur was putting on a very brave front, facing his mortality with a sturdiness that has to be admired. Of course, saying that he had a happiness that 'could not come to any man who had no wife and children' feels very much like a stab at Barrie, even if not meant maliciously. Perhaps in all the care that the Scotsman was giving to him, Arthur was reminded that he was a lucky man to have a whole family that loved him in such a difficult time, something that Barrie had only acquired in people that were in no way blood-related to him. He might've thought that Barrie was utterly miserable,

So the older ones have become glassy-eyed and seldom speak…

and softened against him when he realised that the man just wanted a family to love him in the way that he was prepared to give love. Latching on to the Llewelyn Davies' was not malevolent in any way.

The news that Arthur's cancer was terminal came to Sylvia and to Barrie. Barrie assured Sylvia:

> *'I am thinking of you and Arthur all the time. I am still full of hope.'*[16]

Facing such a dark and definitive end, Sylvia would've admittedly been in a very vulnerable state, but with five sons she was unable to break down or unleash her emotions publicly.

Arthur wrote to his father, the Reverend John Llewelyn Davies:

> *'Whatever may be in store for me, I hope I shall bear it as befits the son of a brave & wise man. I am troubled for myself, but much more for Sylvia. She is brave to a degree that I should have thought hardly possible, busy all day with endless activities & kindnesses for me & for the boys, & all the time the burden is almost heavier than she can bear... I can see the end of what I may have to endure, but she at present seems to face the prospect of endless misery, & only sees that she must go on for the sake of the boys... She & all the boys were never so desirable to me as now, & it is hard if I have to leave them... Barrie's unfailing kindness & tact are a great support to us both...'*[17]

Despite one potential treatment leading the family towards a hopeful outcome and future, it was November of 1906 when Arthur concluded that his artificial jaw was no longer useful to him, and only caused discomfort when he wore it anyway. He was also taking morphia at night for the pain he endured.

Arthur continued to deteriorate over the Christmas period, and all the while *Peter Pan* had started up again at the theatre, with Pauline Chase now starring as Peter. Arthur's sister took the boys to see it, no doubt to keep their spirits up despite the shadows they faced at home.

The success of *Peter Pan* in theatres led to *Hodder and Stoughton* extracting the chapters about Peter from *The Little White Bird* and publishing them as a separate book known as *Peter Pan in Kensington Gardens*. Barrie placed the following dedication at the beginning:

> 'TO SYLVIA AND ARTHUR LLEWELYN DAVIES
> AND THEIR BOYS (MY BOYS)'[18]

The addition at the end of the dedication was no doubt probably a little distasteful at the time since Arthur was fully aware of what and who he was having to leave behind, and seeing such words only would've added a sting to what was already a very emotionally painful time for him.

However, Peter Davies brought up an interesting point in a future letter to Mary Hodgson in 1946:

> *'Would you say that, assuming father never really liked J.M.B., he nevertheless became much fonder of him towards the end, and was much comforted in his last months by the thought that J.M.B.'s money would be there to help mother and all of us after his death?'*[19]

Of course, if Barrie hadn't been around in the way that he was, the future of Sylvia and the boys remains uncertain. Although two good families remained either side of Arthur and Sylvia, what with Gerald du Maurier and his successful family at one end and the esteemed Reverend John Llewelyn Davies at the other, it isn't certain where the boys would've been housed or even if they all could be kept together along with their mother.

In response to Peter, Mary wrote:

> *'Your Father acquiesced to the inevitable, with astounding Grace and Fortitude. It would help your Mother – and further than that he neither desired nor was able to go.'*[20]

In the new year of 1907, Arthur gradually lost the ability to speak entirely. He reverted back to communicating through notes, and among a number that he wrote was one for Barrie:

> '—Dear Jimmy
> -I just like to see you.

So the older ones have become glassy-eyed and seldom speak…

> *-I put all the burdens on you because you can help better than anyone.*
> *-Perhaps better that none of them should see me afterwards? Impression so given never disappears – not the sort of impression one wishes to be permanent.*
> *-Do write more things other than plays.* '21

It's more evidence that Arthur's imminent death had softened him towards Barrie, and witnessing Barrie's intentions to continue caring for the family both physically and financially after he was gone must've consoled him greatly in preparation for leaving them. They were, after all, to be without the person who brought the household an income.

The two were particularly close now – Barrie was always by his bedside, save for a short trip he made to Ireland with Frohman at the end of March for the opening of *Peter Pan* in Dublin.

During this time, Barrie made a number of notes in his personal notebook, including:

> '…*Speaks to a friend (a father) about great difference in dying if you have children (yourself living on) – if you haven't you go out completely.* '22

Here is the main difference Barrie saw between himself and Arthur: being with or without children to carry on their memory and legacy. Arthur had five sons, all with great potential in life, and Barrie had a wife he rarely spent time with and a dog who probably wouldn't live past the age of ten.

By the easter holidays, Arthur knew that he wouldn't be around for much longer and requested that his sons be spared witnessing his final, decaying days. George, Jack, Peter, Michael and Nico were all sent to stay with their grandmother, Emma du Maurier, at Ramsgate. The final letter Arthur managed to write before he passed was to his son, Michael:

> *April 15, 1907*
> *My dearest Michael,*
> *My letters from my boys are indeed a pleasure to me when they arrive in the morning. I hope my boys are getting lots of happiness out of other people's kindness to them and their*

own kindness to other people every day. It would be fine to have a magic carpet and... [fly] to Ramsgate, and see what is going on... I expect you are having plenty of fun and very fine weather, but that we are getting more flowers, especially primroses. My nurse is very good at finding primroses and violets.

Your affectionate Father.[23]

Over at Ramsgate, Peter later spoke of the moments that unfurled when he and his brothers were informed of their father's death:

'...first Jack, and then I, was summoned to Grannie's bedroom... and by her told the news, which she had perhaps just received by telegram. She told us very simply, without circumlocution or excessive emotion, sitting up in bed with (I think) a lace nightcap on; and I believe the meaning of her words penetrated pretty clearly to one's immature brain, though not of course their full and permanent significance. It was, as I remember it, a dull and windy day, and I recollect wandering up to the night nursery and staring out of the window for long minutes in vague wretchedness and gloom, at the grey sea and the distant Gull lightship... for the moment I think it was borne in on me that a disastrous thing had overcome us.'[24]

Chapter 8

"If only you could be this way forever!"
1907–1909

'How he loved us all & he has been taken from us.'[1]

The days following Arthur's death saw many kindnesses from the friends and family around the Llewelyn Davies family. Sylvia revealed in a letter to the family's close friend, Dolly Ponsonby:

'Kind Hugh Macnaghten – a dear friend of Arthur's – is going to have George in his house at Eton in September... I am grateful to many, many friends.'

Of course, she was racked with grief for her husband, taken so young and leaving five sons that were barely even close to reaching adulthood. Dolly related her memories of the time in a letter to Peter in 1946:

'... I have neither before nor since known such anguish as she suffered during his illness. She burst out twice to me about it, but not more – words were inadequate to both of us – and always her reserve about what she cared about was very strong.'[2]

During the initial stages of her grief, Sylvia began the sporadic writings of a will, or at least something highly resembling a will, no doubt shaken by the young age her husband had unexpectedly died. These notes were mostly an internal monologue in no particular order and with little organisation. It ended with:

> 'Of one thing I am certain – that J. M. Barrie (the best friend in the whole world) will always be ready to advise out of his love for'[3]

The sentence ends abruptly here, showing how erratic and emotionally distraught she must've been. Of these notes, particularly how they ended, Peter Davies later commented:

> 'What would the next word or words have been if Sylvia had not stopped writing when she did? Jocelyn? My precious boys?'[4]

Dealing with her own grief was enough, but Sylvia also had to help her five children deal with theirs as well. As a mother, she did her best, but there were of course times when even the simplest of things overwhelmed her. For example, Peter mentioned an occasion in which his mother's emotions became overwhelmed in front of him:

> 'One day George and I were larking about in an intolerable way. Arguing and letting off steam... until poor Sylvia, exasperated beyond endurance, cried out "Oh stop, stop, stop! You know you would never dare behave like this if your father was still alive!"... it is an instance [of] the... heartlessness or thoughtlessness of small boys.'[5]

The boys were only small and dealing with a huge loss at a time where 'boys don't cry' – their only emotional outlets appeared to be carried out with no regard to their mother, when play and roughhousing was all they really had to help them cope and channel their emotions.

Barrie wrote of children being 'gay and innocent and heartless' in *Peter and Wendy*, understanding that the depths of childhood made heartless appearances, but it didn't make a child a bad person. Empathy grows into a person over time, and Barrie saw this in a way that other grown-ups did

"If only you could be this way forever!"

not. He understood at a core level the very make-up of a child, hence his popularity among them as a friend, rather than an elder.

Peter, however, saw it more as a means for control:

> *'There's no denying that, from Arthur's death onwards, he did increasingly "own" Sylvia and her boys after his fashion… with the help of his money, which made generosity an easy business for him…'*[6]

It can't be denied that Barrie was very generous with his money, in a way he did not realise was coming across as a means for control or over the top. To begin with, he took Sylvia and the boys from Egerton House and up to Dhivach Lodge for a holiday in the summer, a house he'd rented in a wooded area behind Loch Ness in Scotland. Barrie most likely thought that being away from the house that held so many fragile memories would help them all to come to terms with life without the man of the house, and to heal from the events leading up to his death.

Mary Barrie was also there for the duration, though the marriage between the Barries was starting to crumble at this point.

As Barrie spent his time fishing and wandering the Scottish countryside with the boys, he also continued his work on *Peter and Wendy*, the novel of the play, by incorporating much of Michael's personality into Peter's character. Michael's nightmares, which were still persisting, are an example of what came to appear in the novel:

> *'Sometimes… [Peter] had dreams, and they were more painful than the dreams of other boys. For hours he could not be separated from these dreams, though he wailed piteously in them.'*[7]

They stayed at the lodge from June to mid-September, when the boys were due back at school.

Upon their return, George started at Eton at the age of fourteen, and seemed to settle in well and quickly according to the regular letters he wrote to his mother, which were a requirement from the school for all pupils. There's no doubt that the change in scenery and new, thorough routine were extremely helpful factors in getting him to thrive despite the loss he'd suffered.

> *'It's not a bad den, and will be able to be fitted up jolly nicely... I have spoken to two or three chaps here already. They are jolly decent. One is called Lord Newton Butler...'* [8]

Meanwhile, Sylvia decided to sell Egerton House. The memories probably proved too much for her, and the expanse of the house and garden must've been daunting to walk alone. She moved to 23 Campden Square, London, in October 1907, and Barrie assisted financially with various costs. Additionally, the house wasn't far from Kensington Gardens, and Leinster Corner where Barrie himself resided with his wife.

Sylvia took Peter, Michael and Nico to stay at Ramsgate with her mother whilst the house was being renovated, where Emma du Maurier was helping to provide support for both Sylvia and the boys.

On 29th November, Barrie wrote in a letter to Sylvia:

> *'Dearest Jocelyn,*
> *Tomorrow I am meaning to go to see George as they have a big 'footer' day, and I am a good deal agitated as to what hat Millington Drake would prefer me to wear. It will probably end (against my better judgement) in my donning the now somewhat PASSÉE bowler... I hope you are all pretty well. When I don't hear I dread you may be ill, but I trust it is not so... I am longing for you to be on Campden Hill. Love to all,*
>
> *Your*
> *J.M.B.'* [9]

Barrie's involvement with the boys was at least a constant that the whole family could rely on, as his eagerness to make sure all was stable with Sylvia portrayed.

Jack, however, was not faring as well as the rest of his brothers in terms of friendship and support. With George at Eton and very popular with many friends, Peter at a school on Orme Square and Michael and Nico starting at Norland Place, Jack was secluded and the furthest away from his family at

"If only you could be this way forever!"

the Royal Navy College in Osborne. His future wife, Geraldine, recounted in later years what he'd told her of it:

> *'... he hated it, he loathed it, he hated it with a deadly loathing. It was pretty awful – the ragging and the bullying that went on was intolerably horrible, and a little boy who had never been away from home was easy meat.'*[10]

Jack didn't inform his mother – or anyone else – of his feelings toward his situation. It's believed that he kept quiet on the subject because he didn't want to add more troubles to an already grieved Sylvia, and was not as close with Barrie as his brothers. His wife commented:

> *'He enormously disliked the idea of this silly little man presuming to take the place of his father.'*[11]

Since these are the words of his wife, we have to assume that Jack's feeling towards Barrie resulted mostly negative, which isn't too surprising coming from a boy who was having to repress the trauma of his father's death and deal with it all alone, away from his family. His family, being the people he should've stayed around to help process his grief.

Nico provided another viewpoint on Jack and his attitude:

> *'Jack more than most could swing emotionally from plus to minus; fundamentally he was very fond of Uncle Jim, tho' there were numerous times when he swung against him, largely caused by his being the loner in the Navy with us other 4 being more constantly under J.M.B.'s eye... Had Jack been to Eton like the rest of us, his attitude to Uncle Jim might have been very different.'*[12]

On the other hand, in the same interview with Geraldine, she was asked if Jack ever changed his attitude at all towards Barrie, or if it was more or less the same? She responded:

> Geraldine: *'More or less the same, I should've thought. We didn't see him so much. We would be in one part of the country and he would be in London.'*

> *Interviewer: 'The impression that's been had from several other people is that he was the one sort of turned against him.'*
> *Geraldine: 'I don't think he did, really, no. Merely he didn't see so much of him because he wasn't there.'* [13]

Furthermore, this completely changes the initial impression people have: the reason Jack wasn't so fond of Barrie wasn't because he openly disliked him, but because he just didn't really know him well after spending so much of his time away.

Nevertheless, this was the point where Jack started to become estranged from his Uncle Jim, and with such a complicated childhood with losing his father, the sudden and intense fame that *Peter Pan* had brought to his family and the relationship the Scottish playwright had with his family, it's no wonder people saw his lack of connection to Barrie as a build-up of resentment.

All these factors would've generated an unending amount of gossip, and with Barrie's divorce now in the light, Jack was probably subjected to having to hear rumours and negative talk of his family as well.

Being a young boy in such a judgmental society was bound to cause a backlash, but many have interpreted this particular situation – without looking at the details – with the notion that Barrie was causing abuse.

The Llewelyn Davies family officially moved into the new house on Campden Hill Square in December 1907. Peter Davies later wrote of it:

> *'And here, I think, Sylvia did succeed, gradually, in regaining something of the zest for life. The boys were a fond amusement and distraction for her, relatives came frequently, and the dog-like J.M.B. still living at Leinster Corner and constantly in attendance... Everything must have been done, by all who had the care of us and above all Sylvia herself, to shut out the imp of sorrow and self-pity from our young lives.'* [14]

Meanwhile, *Peter Pan* once again came to the stage for Christmas.

Barrie had made a couple of changes for the new season, and the inclusion of fairy dust being needed *as well as* happy thoughts in order to fly (at the request of the London Ambulance Service) was put into motion.

"If only you could be this way forever!"

There was also an addition to the end of the play for this one year; a scene involving a grown-up Wendy seeing Peter again and letting her own daughter Jane go off to Neverland with him for spring-cleaning. Tessie Parke, the actress playing the baby mermaid, said in her announcement to the audience when they thought the play had ended:

> *'We are now going to do a new act for the first and only time on any stage... it will never be done again.'*[15]

The scene, later transcribed into prose for the final chapter of *Peter and Wendy*, showed a grown-up Wendy still living in the same house and with a daughter of her own: Jane. Wendy tells her stories of Peter Pan until Jane can recite them better, and of course Peter has not been to visit Wendy in years. On this night, Peter finally makes his return as if no time has passed, much to the shock of Wendy, who is embarrassed to have grown:

> *'He was a little boy, and she was grown up. She huddled by the fire not daring to move, helpless and guilty, a big woman.*
> *'"Hullo, Wendy," he said, not noticing any difference, for he was thinking chiefly of himself; and in the dim light her white dress might have been the nightgown in which he had seen her first.*
> *'"Hullo, Peter," she replied faintly, squeezing herself as small as possible. Something inside her was crying "Woman, Woman, let go of me."'*

When Peter learns that Wendy is no longer a child and has a baby of her own, he is momentarily shocked that time has passed the way it has.

> *'Then she turned up the light, and Peter saw. He gave a cry of pain; and when the tall beautiful creature stooped to lift him in her arms he drew back sharply.*
> *'"What is it?" he cried again.*
> *'She had to tell him.*
> *'"I am old, Peter. I am ever so much more than twenty. I grew up long ago."*
> *'"You promised not to!"*

> *"'I couldn't help it. I am a married woman, Peter.'*
> *"'No, you're not.'*
> *"'Yes, and the little girl in the bed is my baby.'*
> *"'No, she's not.'*

The denial and heartbreak was paramount for Barrie to show in the story so that audiences could see that Peter did not love Wendy romantically, just relied on her role as a stand-in mother. He seems to get over this betrayal very quickly when he thoughtlessly takes Jane's hand so that she may now fly away to Neverland with him instead.

Wendy lets them go in the end – rather reluctantly – and she watches them fly away from the same nursery window that she flew from herself.

> *'As you look at Wendy, you may see her hair becoming white, and her figure little again, for all this happened long ago. Jane is now a common grown-up, with a daughter called Margaret; and every spring cleaning time, except when he forgets, Peter comes for Margaret and takes her to the Neverland... and thus it will go on, so long as children are gay and innocent and heartless.'* [16]

The addition to the story was greeted with a fifteen-minute applause, to which Barrie actually made an appearance on stage to welcome the cheers, something that he'd not done for a performance of *Peter Pan* before. Denis Macktail wrote of the occasion:

> *'In his black overcoat, his scarf, and holding his bowler hat in his hand. He said nothing, the vision was distinctly brief...'* [17]

The new act was such a success with the audience that it was later incorporated into the novel adaptation, but it was never performed on stage again. It showed that you can still believe in the same wonders that you did as a child and pass down the belief of fairies and flying and the like to your children. It provided an ending to Barrie's story that Peter still lived on and would live on through other children, that the magic of Neverland was forever present.

In 1908, Barrie made the trip with Frohman to Paris for the opening of *Peter Pan* at the Vaudeville Theatre. His story about a flying boy who

"If only you could be this way forever!"

wouldn't grow up was reaching international shores much quicker than Barrie ever could've expected; what was it about this play with whimsical themes that fascinated people so much? He was, after all, feeling as if he were that boy himself, unable to feel as grown up as he actually was. That, and he felt completely alone in it.

Some of his innocent immaturity came out in his letters, in which his way of seeing things sound very much as if a child had thought them up. In June, Barrie wrote to Michael for his 8th birthday:

> *'I wish I could be with you and your candles. You can look on me as one of your candles, the one that burns badly – the greasy one that is bent in the middle. But still, hurray, I am Michael's candle... I wish I could see you putting on the redskins clothes for the first time. Won't your mother be frightened... Dear Michael, I am very fond of you, but don't tell anybody.'* [18]

'...but don't tell anybody.' This is a line that can come across as rather sinister or with a hidden meaning, particularly to anyone that hasn't considered Barrie's innocence. However, in a time where men and boys were frowned upon for showing any kind of affection towards each other – whether it be platonic or familial – this is probably more likely the reason for Barrie's wish for secrecy. That, or Barrie didn't want to let on more than people already knew that Michael was his favourite of the Llewelyn Davies boys.

On the other hand, it could be just a playful game of secrets, as children are likely to keep.

Sylvia and her boys spent that summer without Barrie as he was caught up writing his next play, *What Every Woman Knows*. They rented a house in Bournemouth, where Barrie visited them just briefly; any time he could spare for them was time always made. He also called in on Dolly Ponsonby on his way to Black Lake Cottage, where she spoke of the occasion and highlighted Barrie's love for the family he'd merged himself into:

> *'We talked a great deal of Sylvia's boys & it is extraordinary to see how they fill his life & supply all his human interest.'* [19]

Being so close to the family already, any perspective that she gave on Barrie provides us with a good account of his most true character.

It was at this time, the late summer of 1908, that Gilbert Cannan entered Barrie's immediate circle. Cannan was a novelist and dramatist who'd been circling a woman with romantic interest called Kathleen Chase, a sculptor who ended up engaged to Barrie's close friend, Captain Scott. The whole affair caused some upset from misunderstandings within the group, and ultimately Cannan was rather wounded. He found comfort in the Barries' company, but particularly with that of Mary Barrie.

Over the Christmas break of 1908 and 1909, Barrie took Sylvia and the boys on a three-week ski trip to Switzerland. It was his Christmas present to the family, though Mary Barrie was also in attendance. Also there for the trip was Gilbert Cannan.

They stayed at the Grand Hotel at the village of Caux, a relatively remote and mountainous landscape on Lake Geneva – the perfect location to sneak away and isolate yourself. Nico remarked of the time:

> *'...how astonishingly simple/ignorant = unknowing Barrie was about what went on around him in the so-to-speak dirty things of the world... He frequently employed a safety-curtain which he would pull down between his own mind and the facts of life in the world around him.'*[20]

It was blatantly obvious to almost everyone present on the trip that Mary Barrie and Gilbert Cannan were spending more than the usual amount of time that two friends might together, and that they were also particularly fond of one another.

In such a time, gossip was safer than confrontation since not a word was said to Barrie about the subject, nor was he questioned about the suspicion. According to a later allegation by Cannan, Sylvia apparently 'encouraged his affair with Mary Barrie' and made it easy for them to meet and see each other unknown to Barrie.

Even Jack, just thirteen at the time, was documented to say:

> *"Why is Mr Cannan always with Mrs Barrie?"*[21]

Barrie did not record much on the matter. Whether he knew but didn't want to confront his wife or was actually oblivious to the situation since

"If only you could be this way forever!"

it concerned a romantic matter, there is no evidence to show for or against either possibility.

Perhaps Barrie did know. There's a chance that he saw this as his opportunity to finally get out of the marriage he was socially pressured to commit to, though that doesn't explain why Mary's affair stayed in the shadows for so long.

Towards the end of the holiday in Switzerland, Sylvia started to become unwell. Peter described her to be 'suffering great pain', and:

> *'From this time forward Sylvia, though sometimes better for shorter or longer periods, was never completely well.'*[22]

One unspoken theory is that Sylvia's heartbreak was the leading cause of her demise, and although she did her best to see her children through their own lives, the loss of her husband was too much for her to bear.

However, upon the family's return home, life continued on as normal for Sylvia and her sons; around Easter, she took them all to Ramsgate to visit their grandmother, Emma du Maurier, a regular family trip. Barrie, meanwhile, was held up at Black Lake Cottage with Gilbert Cannan, who was now a member of the Dramatic League – an organisation of which Barrie was a founding member. They were working on setting up a National Theatre in England.

Additionally, Barrie was in conversation with the sculptor Sir George Frampton to commission a Peter Pan statue. He gave Sir George the photographs taken of Michael dressed as Peter when at Ramsgate to be the primary model, immortalising his original idea of what the character should convey when set in stone. It gives cause to wonder whether this was to actually immortalise the character of Peter Pan, or Michael in his golden years of childhood.

Barrie remained modest as the popularity around his most famous play grew, however. He didn't enjoy the attention of his audiences and when he was offered a knighthood, he turned it down. His main focus remained transfixed upon Sylvia and her boys. In missing them, Barrie wrote to her in June:

> *'How I wish I were going down to see Michael and Nicholas... I feel they are growing up without my looking on... I can't*

> *picture a summer day that does not have Michael skipping on in front. That is summer to me. And all the five know me as nobody else does.* '23

He truly was clinging to them for his happiness, and with his Scottish roots being mostly dwindled, they were now the only family he really knew.

Six months had passed since the holiday in Switzerland, and July 1909 was when Mary and Gilbert Cannan's affair was fully uncovered to Barrie. Mr Hunt, the gardener at Black Lake Cottage, in a moment of anger from an incident where the lady of the house had scolded him, told his master that all the staff were aware of the true nature of the relationship between Mary and Cannan – and had known since November 1908. The pair had been at the cottage without Barrie, so were able to act a little more freely around each other.

As soon as the news was broken to him, Barrie went straight to London and telegraphed his wife to meet him immediately. When finally confronted, Mary simply said, 'It is all quite true.' Perhaps she was also just waiting for it all to come out, and saw it as the best means of leaving her marriage; being careless in her affair was not an accident.

Barrie and Mary went to visit their friend and solicitor, Sir George Lewis, in the aftermath, where Barrie said the following:

> *'My wife said it was the only time it had ever taken place, and they had both been in a state about it. I said, 'If you will come back I will forgive you. No one would ever know anything about it;' She said it would all be pretence. I should be thinking of her all the time, but he was the only person in the world... to her... She said that it would be a much more ignoble thing to go back to me in those circumstances.'* '24

Divorce was rare and a scandal in the Edwardian era, so Barrie airing the offer of return for Mary could've been a front in order to maintain his image. On the other hand, maybe he was genuinely sad to be losing a companion – in the very least, she had been a constant in his life for over ten years. Either way, it only seemed fair to release Mary from the marriage – a marriage he was never fully invested in anyway – and despite his offers for her to stay with him and avoid scandal, she insisted upon their separation.

"If only you could be this way forever!"

As a result, Barrie went to stay with A. E. W. Mason, an author and politician, in his London flat where he was recorded by Mason to:

> '... walk up and down, up and down all night in his heavy boots until the sound of it drove everyone within hearing almost as frantic as the miserable little figure itself.' [25]

The prospect of the divorce – or more likely the betrayal in retrospect – must've caused some distress to the man, considering he'd also been working so closely with Gilbert Cannan.

Barrie and Mason went to Switzerland for a time soon after.

Meanwhile, Mary wrote to H.G. Wells, another well-known author, about the state of things with her soon-to-be ex-husband:

> 'He seems to have developed the most ardent passion for me now that he has lost me... he says he knows I would be happier with G.C. and that we ought to marry, one moment, and the next clamours for me.' [26]

Being apart had new meaning for them and reflecting on the events seemed to have Mary feeling some remorse.

Some people claimed that Mary had had multiple lovers prior to being caught with Cannan and was just looking for an escape from her marriage, whilst others witnessed two people genuinely in love. Ultimately, it was stated that Mary did love her husband, but more in the way a mother might love her child.

Despite her causing Barrie emotional pain, Mary did still care for him; it's likely that she felt immense guilt for how she had brought the marriage to an end, even if there had clearly been no happiness between them for a long time.

In 1904, the Barrie's had celebrated ten years of marriage; their Tin Wedding Anniversary. Notes Barrie made in his personal notebook the following day were highlighted in underlines so forcefully that the pencil had actually pushed through the page.

> 'Idea – Husband & wife story, scene caused by husband – evidently they don't get on well together – his fault – she violent – interrupted by visitors with Tin Wedding presents (He

> *hasn't remembered it is their wedding day.) She immediately in woman's way sort of manner talks as if husband best in world – how he spoils her, &c, pretends grand present from him, &c. When they're gone, he remorseful & swears to make it happy day yet for her (thinks he's doing finely) then she shows true self – says can quarrel over little things… but not over the big things. Too late to talk of love & his giving it to her, she no longer wants it. Her own love for him has gone from her, spilt, ended &c… She says he can have affairs with other women as he wills. They don't disturb her. Do as he likes about that. Wd like to go on pretending to people happy &c, less for his sake (he had thought it all so touching & all for him)…* '[27]

With so much of the text reflecting factual aspects of the time, it's likely that these notes were based on a very real scene that occurred. The conversation about having affairs with other women could've been something that came up in an argument between Barrie and Mary, though this is not proven as fact.

When Barrie returned from Switzerland in the autumn of 1909, he was able to take Michael along to his first day at Wilkinson's. Still being there as Uncle Jimmy for his boys took a priority despite the impending court date for his divorce. Sylvia had little to say about the situation, but with the claims from Cannan that she'd encouraged the affair in so many words and actions, she probably believed the outcome to be for the best. It couldn't have been a ploy to ensure more financial aid from Barrie, since his actions thus far had already concluded that his support for her and the boys would never dissipate.

On 13th October, Barrie's divorce case took place. In support of their friend, fellow writers to Barrie wrote to every editor in Fleet Street to request they not exploit Barrie's divorce 'as a mark of respect and gratitude to a writer of genius'. In the end, only *The Daily Telegraph*, *Daily Mail* and *Daily Mirror* covered the story.

COURT TRANSCRIPT:

> *BERNARD: Towards the end of July this year Mr Hunt made a communication to you as to what happened the previous November?*
>
> *BARRIE: Yes.*

"If only you could be this way forever!"

BERNARD: What did he tell you?

BARRIE: He said his wife took up tea in the morning to Mr Cannan, and he was not in his room. She then went with tea to my wife's room and knocked and heard my wife saying, 'Gilbert, Gilbert!' She then returned to Mr Cannans room and entered it. He was not there and the bed had not been slept in.

...

BERNARD: Did you then offer to separate by deed if she would promise to have nothing more to do with him?

BARRIE: Yes.

BERNARD: And she refused?

BARRIE: Yes.[28]

It was also apparently revealed in court that the marriage had never been consummated. Once again, the theory that Barrie was asexual appears the most likely reason for the lack of physical affection and sexual contact between him and his wife.

Mary said in a letter to H.G. Wells of the divorce case:

> '[Barrie] came out badly in court. 3 lies. First, never said it was the only time. 2nd. It is my cottage, lease is in my name and I bought it with my money. 3rd. It is seven years since we separated and that does not spell happiness...'[29]

Barrie was clearly very bitter in the way a child might be jealous of another child taking his toys. He didn't appear to act very maturely, nor react in the way that most upset adults would, and his emotions to the situation got the best of him when formally suing on the grounds of infidelity.

Mary, in her defence, never once pulled Sylvia's name into the divorce discussions. After years of watching her husband dote over another woman, even if there was no romantic intention, perhaps it was her lack of proof that prevented her from bringing the Llewelyn Davies family into the affair. Or it could've just been her last kindness to Barrie, and a willingness to get through the divorce as swiftly as possible.

Shortly after the case was settled, Barrie moved into his own flat in Adelphi Terrace House, which was a much further walk to Kensington Gardens and closer to the River Thames.

Two days after the divorce between Barrie and Mary was finalised, Sylvia collapsed on the stairs at home.

AN AFTERTHOUGHT OF WHAT BECAME OF MARY ANSELL AND GILBERT CANNAN

Mary Ansell and Gilbert Cannan married in 1910, and despite Mary's continued wish to have children they didn't have any. In fact, their marriage was not a particularly happy one.

Cannan had an affair with their maid, Gwen Wilson, in 1917, and she became pregnant with his child. Cannan and Ansell ended their marriage the following year, and Cannan moved in with Wilson and her new husband, Henry Mond, in a ménage à trois arrangement.

Meanwhile, Mary had to provide for herself entirely again and started working for the war effort. She helped pack medical supplies and rolled bandages to get by, but Barrie came to hear of her struggling circumstances and set out looking for her. He offered to help her financially – a generous move after the divorce and seeing her remarry – which she accepted.

Barrie gave her an annual allowance which she received until his death, and even then he left her a bequest of £1000 as well as an annuity of £600. When assessing the inflation rate from 1937 to 2022, this is the equivalent of receiving approximately £86,429 in total.

Cannan was not so fortunate in his fate. Following the First World War, he tried to get back into his main line of work – writing – but suffered a mental breakdown in 1923. He was committed to the Priory Hospital in Roehampton as a mental patient, before being transferred to Holloway Sanatorium near Virginia Water. He remained there for the rest of his life, dying of cancer on 30th June 1955.

Chapter 9

Never is an awfully long time
1909–1910

Peter was at home when his mother collapsed on the stairs, along with Mary Hodgson.

> *'I happened to be about... and Mary Hodgson, red-faced and agitated, tended her and shooed me away, not before I had received an impression of direness and fatality, and a sense of shocked misery and half-comprehending desolation, which has remained with me ever since.'*[1]

The family's doctor, Doctor Rendel, came to the house upon their call, and after his examination of Sylvia he was noted to say that whatever was wrong with Sylvia was very serious, and that nothing should be said to the family.

Perhaps he wanted to make sure his suspicions were confirmed before notifying anyone of Sylvia's illness, so when a specialist was called, who said it was 'too close to the heart to operate' – it was confirmed that Sylvia too had fallen victim to cancer.

Despite the confident diagnosis, there was an insistence of secrecy that in modern times would be considered illegal. According to Mary Hodgson in a later letter to Peter, everyone was kept almost entirely in the dark and hushed to silence:

> *'It was impressed on me that your Mother – on no account – was to talk about her illness to me & that at all costs she must not know how ill she was. Life was to go on as usual and the Boys were just to be told Mother had to stay in bed and rest for a long time.'*[2]

Horrifyingly, even Sylvia herself was not aware of how bad her own illness really was. To keep such a life-changing fact from a person about their own health is most definitely inhumane, and shocking to know when it's remembered how Sylvia had five young boys – already without a father – she needed to provide for.

Even Sylvia's eldest sister, Beatrice (known as Trixie), was unbeknownst to the cancer. She wrote of Sylvia in a letter to Marie (known as May), the middle sister between them:

> *'But I am not surprised, she never seemed to rest at all, & I expect when holidays come is quite tired out – at her age and after all she went through with Arthur it was bound to come to something, but I hope a rest will show improvement.'*[3]

It's very likely that Sylvia's illness was brought about by the distress and trauma of losing her husband. It's common, even in the modern day, for people to develop severe and even terminal illnesses from stress and upsetting life events, and along with the pressure to bring up five boys without Arthur, Sylvia must've been in a state of tumultuous grief.

To put it bluntly, Sylvia was dying of heartbreak.

When George and Jack returned home for Christmas in 1909, Sylvia was mostly restricted to her bed. She had a nurse to help tend to her – Nurse Loosemore – whom Mary Hodgson butted heads with on multiple occasions, but they both came to the same conclusion about the young Llewelyn Davies boys.

They hoped that Sylvia might show some improvement with the life and joy the boys would bring to the house when they returned. With a less sombre environment, it might bring the colour back to her cheeks and the mobility back in her body. However, even though the attendance of her sons improved her general mood, by spring 1910 she was having to use a bath-chair as well.

There was no intention made by doctors to operate, which although was disheartening it meant that she was at least able to maintain her presence at home. Barrie once again made his constant vigil at her side apparent, helping care for her and assist in anything the boys might need; he must've been quite alarmed at the sudden decline of Sylvia's health, and the prospect that his boys were about to be orphaned.

Above: The cottage in Kirriemuir where Barrie was born and raised. (Courtesy of the author's collection)

Right: James Barrie, aged 12 in 1872. (Courtesy of The Barrie Archives)

Barrie's mother, Margaret Ogilvy in 1872.
(Courtesy of The Barrie Archives)

James Barrie in 1882 aged 22, Edinburgh University.
(Courtesy of The Barrie Archives)

Barrie in 1892, two years before his marriage to Mary Ansell.

Mary Ansell, circa 1890, around the time her and Barrie were married. (Alamy)

Left: The Barries' dog, Porthos, in 1899. (Courtesy of The Barrie Archives)

Below left and below right: Arthur and Sylvia in 1890, the year after they met. (Courtesy of the Walter Beinecke Rare Book and Manuscript Library, Yale University)

Above: Sylvia with George and Jack in 1895. (Courtesy of the Walter Beinecke Rare Book and Manuscript Library, Yale University)

Below: George, Jack and Peter photographed by Barrie as *The Boy Castaways of Black Lake Island*, at Black Lake Cottage in 1899. (Courtesy of the Walter Beinecke Rare Book and Manuscript Library, Yale University)

Left: Mary Hodgson in 1897, at the time she entered service with the Llewelyn Davies family as a nursery maid. (Courtesy of The Barrie Archives)

Below: Peter Pan's Kensington Gardens Map, as it appears in *The Little White Bird*. (Alamy)

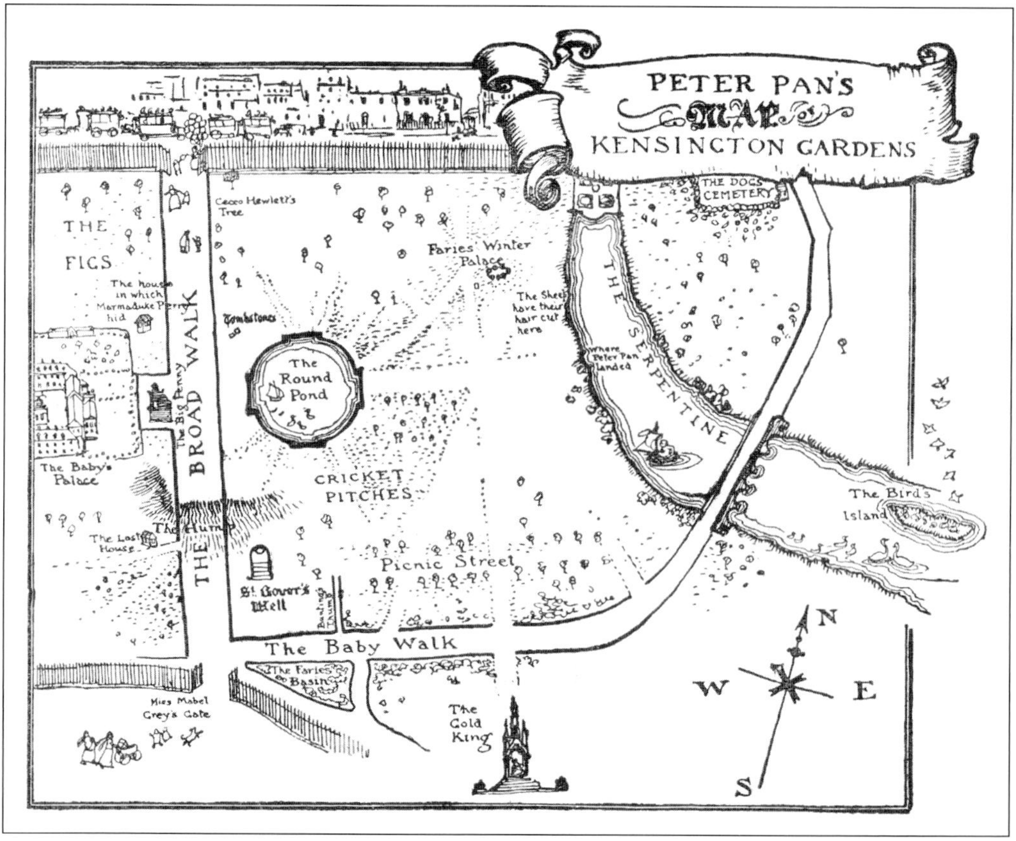

Above: Costumes and artwork from the first London stage production of Peter Pan, showcased at Barrie's birthplace in Kirriemuir, Scotland. (Courtesy of the author's collection)

Below: Barrie and Michael playing; Barrie as Captain Hook and Michael as Peter Pan. Rustington, August 1906. (Alamy)

Above: Arthur Llewelyn Davies and the five boys, 1905. (Alamy)

Left: Michael dressed as Peter Pan in 1906 at Rustington. He was supposed to be the model for the character's statue, but according to Barrie it does not show 'the devil in Peter'. (Alamy)

Statue of Peter Pan close-up – not bearing much of a resemblance to Michael Llewelyn Davies or representing 'the devil in Peter'. (Courtesy of the author's collection)

Full statue of Peter Pan in Kensington Gardens, London. (Courtesy of the author's collection)

Barrie and his second dog, a Newfoundland called Luath, in 1904. (Courtesy of the Walter Beinecke Rare Book and Manuscript Library, Yale University)

Barrie and Michael in 1912. (Courtesy of the Walter Beinecke Rare Book and Manuscript Library, Yale University)

Jack in his Royal Navy Cadet Uniform in 1912. (Courtesy of the Walter Beinecke Rare Book and Manuscript Library, Yale University)

George in Paris in 1914. (Courtesy of the Walter Beinecke Rare Book and Manuscript Library, Yale University)

Peter in 1917, possibly taken on his leave for shell shock. (Courtesy of the Walter Beinecke Rare Book and Manuscript Library, Yale University)

Michael in 1919. (Courtesy of the Walter Beinecke Rare Book and Manuscript Library, Yale University)

Michael and Nico circa 1920. (Courtesy of the Walter Beinecke Rare Book and Manuscript Library, Yale University)

Above: Movie still from Paramount's *Peter Pan* (1924).

Below: Barrie in his flat in Adelphi Terrace, 1930. (Courtesy of the Walter Beinecke Rare Book and Manuscript Library, Yale University)

Right: Barrie with Nico's wife Mary, holding Laura, their daughter, in 1928.

Below: Barrie's grave in Kirriemuir, Scotland. He was buried with his parents and other close family members. (Courtesy of the author's collection)

Above: Rachel Hurd-Wood and Jeremy Sumpter in a still from Universal's Peter Pan (2003). (Alamy)

Below: Jason Isaacs and Richard Briers in a still from Universal's Peter Pan (2003). (Alamy)

Never is an awfully long time

His ultimate mother-figure was decaying right before him.

Despite the lack of conversation about Sylvia's condition in the house, the boys were obviously aware that something was more than wrong with their mother. She was, after all, still a woman only just in her forties, without the ability to move around on her own or care for herself. In one of his letters from Eton, George wrote:

> 'How are you? You never say anything about how you're getting on.... How soon shall you go out in your bath-chair? I do hope I'll be able to wheel you on leave...'[4]

His anxiety is apparent with his proclamation that Sylvia doesn't speak of her illness, though she herself didn't even know what was wrong with her. Being away from her and trying to concentrate on his studies couldn't have made things any easier, either, especially with the gaps of time between seeing her in which he would've noticed her decline in health more prominently.

He was, at least, thriving at Eton; Barrie visited him in the summer of 1910 when Sylvia was too ill to attend herself. Not only was he doing well in his studies but Barrie noted just how popular he was with his fellow pupils and also his teachers. George was now sixteen, and one contemporary said of him:

> 'It was quite extraordinary – almost unique in my experience – for someone quite so successful. He was a tremendous blood at Eton, but you'd never have known it. He wasn't a great talker, but he had great charm. He was rather shy, rather reserved, but his sense of humour was exquisite.'[5]

In many ways, these traits seemed to resemble his Uncle Jimmy a little. It must be noted that Barrie probably noticed this and felt once more that George was almost like his own son that he'd had good influence over. Considering he'd been in the young boy's life since he was just four years old, it makes sense that George picked up some of his Uncle Jimmy's ways.

Michael, meanwhile, wasn't holding up so well. He was recorded on one occasion by George du Maurier to be sitting in the corner of Sylvia's bedroom, doing his homework at the little desk and crying softly. The recent death of his father had probably made him more consciously aware of his parent's mortality, and it may have seemed like time was repeating itself with the downward direction his mother was clearly headed with her ill health.

And no amount of stories about magical fairies and a boy that could fly would be consolation enough.

Peter was due to join George at Eton later that year, and Barrie probably thought that it would do them both good to have a brother nearby with everything that was going on with Sylvia. He intended to finance Peter's place there as he'd promised upon Arthur's death, but Peter instead got himself in through a scholarship. Although this could be interpreted as an action that was done out of stubbornness – to prove that he didn't need the famous writer's help to succeed – it's more likely that Peter's capabilities were starting to shine through, and with his mother's illness clouding his family's lives, his studies would've provided a great distraction.

By July, the secrecy around Sylvia's illness was getting to her. She knew something was very, very wrong with her; her decline in health was rapid to the point of being unable to take care of herself at all, yet both her doctors and family were insisting that there was nothing wrong beyond the norm.

As a result, she hatched a plan to try and extract the truth of her condition from her doctors and Mary Hodgson (who must've known about the diagnosis of cancer by now). Sylvia suggested a holiday with her sons down in Devon. More particularly, in a location that would be far from any neighbour and most specifically, any doctor.

Such seclusion from any medical assistance in her condition would be a huge risk.

Sylvia's mother, Emma du Maurier, was of course horrified by the idea when she heard of it. Her daughter needed full-time assistance and care as well as a doctor on hand should she deteriorate.

Mary Hodgson recalled how:

> *'Dr R[endel] said, "If Sylvia wishes to go, she should have what she wishes." Nurse L[oosemore] said Dr R and J.M.B. were quite mad & eventually told me to make myself & the boys scarce on the journey "as anything might happen".'* [6]

So, they went. And Ashton Farm was indeed a desolate location in the valley of the River Oare, with the nearest village being several kilometers away. For the family to get there from London, it took a five-hour train and then a fifteen-mile car ride, which was obviously a completely exhausting journey for everyone, but especially for the unwell Sylvia.

With Sylvia, her boys and Mary Hodgson set up in the house, Barrie took up residence in some rooms at the nearby village, whilst Emma du Maurier travelled down to stay in the spare room and be close to her daughter.

Everyone settled into the mirage holiday and time slipped into August, the days being much the same as each other. The boys fished in the local waters, a great distraction from the darkness within the house, whilst Barrie appeared by Sylvia's bedside every day. In future years, Mary wrote to Peter:

> '...I only saw your mother at odd times. I think the powers-that-be thought I was not to be trusted...'[7]

At this point, it seemed that not even Sylvia's inner circle were privy to her condition, and Mary must've been a little hurt by this considering she'd been with the family since the eldest of the boys were small. Seeing Barrie, a man who'd stumbled into their lives after her, being allowed in Sylvia's presence when she was not, was a stab in the back for her.

Dolly Ponsonby visited the family on their holiday, and came to say of the occasion:

> 'I think she was in a black gown, and lying on the sofa. I realized then that she was not going to live, and I remember going back and telling my husband, and weeping.'[8]

Emma du Maurier continued to express her concern for her daughter's distance from any doctor. She wrote to May, her middle daughter, about these worries:

> 'It is terrible to think dear Sylvia is so far from doctors... This ought never to have been taken. Today Sylvia is staying in bed, she seems quite to wish to. She seems glad I have come and hopes I can stay and of course I shall, but you can imagine what I feel.'[9]

Finally, on 5th August, a doctor was arranged to come and stay with them at the house. Sylvia was reported to be very upset by the decision to see Doctor Spicer move into the bubble she'd purposefully created:

> '...she was angry and then began to cry, and said "I believe I am very ill"...'[10]

It has to be stated that it was a very cruel action to continue lying to Sylvia, especially at this stage when she was technically reaching end-of-life care, and it's unknown why that decision was made. With the kind of movements going on around her, however, Sylvia didn't need words at this point.

Knowing she was facing death, she dared not be away from her sons for long periods of time. Sylvia now faced the fact that she would not – just like her husband – live to see them grow and become men.

> '...She doesn't wish the boys ever to be kept away from her; of course they are out all day until tea time, and when they are in the garden she can see them... However too many of them soon tire her. Dear Nicholas is very good but of course he is lively and wants to jump about and climb on the backs of others and all that is too much in her room.'[11]

Barrie, Mary, and Emma du Maurier did their best to keep the boys entertained as well as high-spirited whilst also rotating duties on the various needs for Sylvia.

Peter later recalled:

> 'In the evenings we would take the day's catch of small trout in to show Sylvia, as she lay, so much frailer than we knew, on a sofa or in her bed... Sylvia weakened rapidly, and I think she never again left her room.'[12]

It was at this point that it's believed Sylvia attempted – in her very weakened state – to write another will. It wouldn't be found for almost another year, but it was estimated to have been drawn up around this time.

She expressed for the house at Campden Hill Square to be kept as long as possible for her sons, and for them to continue to be under the care of

Mary Hodgson. She elected several trustees and guardians for her boys, including Barrie, her mother, brother, and Arthur's brother Crompton. She also wrote:

> *'I do not wish any of my dear boys to look at me when I am dead – it is a great mistake I think – let them remember me at my best & when I could look at them – that must have been the best time always because I love them so utterly... I do not want any of my boys to go to my funeral, nor do I want it made into a long gloomy day for them.'*[13]

Of course, since her will wasn't found until after all this was to take place, her wishes were sadly never to be fulfilled.

She additionally wrote that she wished to be cremated and buried with Arthur at Hampstead, so the thought of at least being able to join her husband must've been the only comfort for her in being so close to death.

> *'I would like Mama to go over my letters in case anything has to be kept – otherwise I would like everything burnt.'*[14]

Why she wished for her remaining letters to be burnt isn't really known. It could be suggested that something of a scandal hid amongst them, but with no subsequent witness evidence, nothing can be proved. Otherwise, it's a natural wish for privacy when death would take her control of such documents.

It was the 27th August 1910, when Peter recalled the day:

> *'...Nurse Loosemore told us [Sylvia] was not well enough to see us, as she usually did before we went off on our various activities, but that she sent us all her love and would see us in the evening. Jack went off in the car to Minehead... to play golf and I set out on our usual all day fishing expedition. I question whether any of us, even George, the eldest and much the most intimate with J.M.B., felt more than a vague sense of oppression – certainly no clear forebodings.'*[15]

Even then, when it was clear to everyone else that Sylvia was living her final days, the boys didn't seem to quite accept the fact that she was actually going to die.

It was also on that morning that Sylvia saw her reflection in a hand-mirror and was recorded to have said:

"Don't let the boys see me again."[16]

A brave and honourable kindness to her children was made then, as Sylvia faced her end bravely, with her mother and Barrie both by her side.

Emma du Maurier related her daughter's final moments in a letter to May, written the same afternoon as Sylvia's passing:

'...the doctor was holding dear Sylvia's hands and asked me to fan her, but I didn't know the end was so near. She was breathing with great difficulty and I couldn't bear to look at her, then they called in Mr Barrie and I saw what it was and it was all over in about ¼ of an hour. It was her breathing that was exhausted, not heart failure. The doctor, nurse, Mr Barrie and I were the only ones in the room... Darling Sylvia looked perfectly lovely – so calm and happy, and those who love her can only be thankful she is at peace.'[17]

The boys were out at the time, and Peter recalled the afternoon when he made his way back to the house by himself:

'As I went in at the gate, it struck me that there was something peculiar in the aspect of the house: in every window the blinds had been drawn. Somehow or other the dreadful significance of this sombre convention conveyed itself to my shocked understanding, and with heart in boots and unsteady knees I covered the remaining thirty or forty yards to the front door. There J.M.B. awaited me: a distraught figure, arms hanging limp, hair disheveled, wild-eyed.

'In what exact words he told me what I had no need to be told, I forget; but it was brokenly, despairingly, without any pretense of philosophy or resignation or the stiff upper lip.

He must have been sunk in depths far below all that, poor Jimmy... I remember, and I wish I didn't, sobbing out "Mother! Mother!" at intervals during the sad and painful scene... I am almost sure... that I went in to look my last on Sylvia as she lay dead in the room on the ground floor which had been made into her bedroom... confused, unhappy, frightened, looking and yet not looking at the pale, lifeless features, and then of escaping to I know not what limbo to some remote corner of the house... '[18]

Sylvia never wanted her boys to see her once she'd passed, but the grief of the household had been in too much of a disarray to consider this, and the turmoil had everyone stricken.

Barrie himself had just lost perhaps the only woman he had ever really felt some kind of romantic love for, or at least what he understood as romantic love. To him, Sylvia was in the very least the ultimate feminine figure that encompassed womanhood and motherhood so completely and perfectly. Having dealt with so much personal loss throughout his life, this was another blow that led Barrie to make some odd decisions in the aftermath.

First of all, the five Llewelyn Davies boys had to be informed of their mother's passing, and Barrie took it upon himself to break it to each of them as they arrived brokenly back at the house.

According to Barrie, Michael had acted angrily, throwing a tantrum and speaking words of fury. This is an understandable reaction for a boy of just ten years old, especially since he and his brothers were now officially orphans.

Meanwhile, Nico was so young (being only six years of age) that it took him some time to understand and comprehend that his mother was gone forever, whilst George's reaction remains unrecorded. At seventeen, he would've at least been aware that he and his brothers were now in an unstable position in society with no parents, save for the assistance of extensive surrounding family and of course, their Uncle Jimmy.

When Jack was told, he recalled:

'...I was taken into a room where [Barrie] was alone and he told me she was dead. He also told me, which angered me even

then, that Mother had promised to marry him and wore his ring. Even then I thought if it was true it must be because she knew she was dying. I was then taken in to see her and left with her for a bit. She looked quite natural, as she'd always been so pale, very lovely and asleep.'[19]

This was the first anyone had ever heard of an engagement between Barrie and Sylvia. It was mostly suspicious because of how obviously dedicated Sylvia had been to Arthur, even after his death, so the idea of her agreeing to an engagement to the playwright could only have been down to a concern for her son's futures, financially speaking. However, since Barrie had already promised (and proved) his aid to them, it doesn't seem plausible that she would marry him to secure what was already so firmly in place.

Therefore, it's more likely that Barrie made this up more out of concern for the boys, since it was not confirmed where they would now live outside of any school boardings. Barrie probably wanted to make sure that they all be kept together, at a time where they would need it most, and in his desperate love for them did all he could to ensure the best for them.

Even so, this was clearly the wrong thing to say immediately after informing Jack that his mother was dead. Based on Jack's reaction and feelings towards it, this was an insensitive move on Barrie's part, even with his own grief put into consideration. Jack, after all, was on the cusp of sixteen, and already harbouring potential feelings of resentment towards Barrie.

When Nico married in 1926, Barrie gave his new wife a ring which he claimed he'd given to Sylvia, saying that they would have been married had she not become ill and passed away.

It's therefore also possible that it was a fantasy Barrie had made up over the years, more as a fulfilment to his wishes of fatherhood than to actually marry for love; being Sylvia's husband would give him the automatic right to step-fatherhood and all the custodies that came with it.

Overall, there was no other evidence beyond Barrie's word of a secret engagement, so we have to conclude that it wasn't the truth. Peter said of this:

'J.M.B. was quite capable of imagining, and of coming in the end to believe, such a might-have-been... there must have been

conversations between them... about the future, and about what they were to each other; and she may well have given him the thought of marriage – if it could be called that – to play with... But I think that to Jack... the thought was intolerable and even monstrous; so much so that he could not refrain from expressing himself in the most forcible manner to that effect when J.M.B. in an unguarded moment spoke to him of it. To me too, the idea of such a marriage is repugnant.'[20]

Ultimately, the five boys were now without both of their parents, all within the space of just a few years. Their interests and welfare had to be at the forefront of priorities for those around them, and Barrie was at least determined to step up as the protector he always saw himself as to them.

Chapter 10

They are the eyes a mother leaves behind to guard her children
1910–1912

The 28th of August 1910 – just twenty-four hours after Sylvia's death – saw George and Peter walking out to the local village to break the news of their mother's passing via telegram. Various ones were sent to family members, friends, and members of society they were acquainted with, which was a rather morbid job thrust upon Sylvia's still-young sons. Despite being the oldest of the five boys, and it being a respectable act for them to be the ones to carry out this morose task, it was a lot for adolescents to carry emotionally.

Peter recalled:

> 'As we walked down the hill on this gloomy errand... George remarked to me, perhaps merely speaking his thoughts aloud,... that in spite of the tragedy that had come upon us, we seemed to have got up and washed and tied our ties and put on our boots and eaten our breakfast all right: that it wasn't, in fact, the end of the world. Life went on... I knew quite well that he was feeling things at least as deeply as I was myself. But he was the eldest brother, and felt his responsibility.'[1]

George, bravely, saw his position as the new head of the family, and provided what comfort he could in this moment to his younger brother amidst his own grief, at a time when male on male affection was seen as a weakness – even between two brothers who were now orphaned.

A solemn walk with the purpose of sending out the news of a mother's passing would be a core memory for anyone, and not a pleasant one. Barrie

> They are the eyes a mother leaves behind to guard her children

wasn't able to save them from the sadness they now encountered with tales of fairies and pirates and an island where all manner of adventures could happen. The years of their innocence was over; anyone that's encountered tragedy at a young age would be able to account.

For the remaining few weeks of the summer holidays, Mary Hodgson remained at Ashton Farm with Michael and Nico, which may have been another morose decision on the adult's part since it wasn't their home and would only be associated with the location of Sylvia's death. Perhaps it would've made more sense for all the boys to return to the comfort of home at Campden Hill Square where they held mostly happy memories, but only George, Jack and Peter were sent back to London along with Barrie. The reasoning for this decision was because Michael and Nico were deemed too young.

Barrie and the three eldest Llewelyn Davies boys escorted their mother's coffin on the train, and Jack later said to his wife of the journey:

> *'...every time the train stopped at a station, Barrie got out of the carriage and stood with bowed head in front of the guard's van where the coffin was, draped in purple cloth, as if he was on sentry-duty.'* [2]

Jack, already angry at Barrie's claim of an engagement to his mother as well as a general feeling of distance between him and the writer, probably felt that these actions were very dramatic, over the top and completely unnecessary. With Jack being a young boy dealing with so much this is an understandable reaction, particularly when his childhood wasn't the most normal with the drop into the spotlight from *Peter Pan*.

For Barrie, however, this might've been his way of coming to terms with Sylvia's death and what was to come. He was a writer and a creator, he lived in magical worlds he'd fabricated in his head, so it makes sense for him to have been a little theatrical. Mostly, this author believes that it was a genuine coping mechanism for the loss of a woman whom he truly loved, respected, and admired. Although likely not a romantic love, it was still a deep fondness that he hadn't even felt for his ex-wife, and these moments to himself would've been rare now that he was the main guardian of the five young boys Sylvia had left behind.

Back in London, George, Jack, and Peter attended Sylvia's funeral with Barrie. From the ordeal of the time, Peter later said he didn't remember very much of the day, which psychologists today would put down to the brain's way of protecting itself from remembering bad times. Instead, Peter more vividly recalled the following day where Barrie took the three of them to a shop in Haymarket to purchase new fishing rods to use down in Devon; Barrie seemed to think that another trip away would distract them from the recent tragedy, and they were to remain with him until the new school year started anyway.

Peter confirmed from his memories of the trip:

> *'At any rate one seems to remember quite enjoying oneself, flogging the little upland streams and hauling out the little trout, and putting the lowly worm behind one forever.'*[3]

Come September, all the boys started new terms at Eton and Wilkinson's, throwing them back into normality so soon after their mother's death. Continuing life for them as naturally as possible would've at least provided them with a daily structure to keep them in the present and focused on the future as well. Mary Hodgson continued to care for them in the family home, and with no boys around, Barrie took the opportunity to turn back to his writing.

Months passed, and Sylvia's will was finally uncovered. Amongst the other requests she'd made that had been read too late – not letting the boys see her dead body or attend her funeral – there is some controversy over what was actually written concerning the following passage of her will:

> *'What I wd like wd be if Jenny wd come to Mary & that the two together would be looking after the boys & the house & helping each other. And it would be so nice for Mary.'*[4]

Jenny was Mary Hodgson's sister, but it was apparent by now that Jenny had made no such appearance to help with caring for the Llewelyn Davies boys.

What seemed to have happened was, when Barrie transcribed Sylvia's will, 'Jenny' was rewritten to 'Jimmy', which obviously sparked some

They are the eyes a mother leaves behind to guard her children

anger when the change was realised. Obviously, Sylvia was very ill and unaware of her certain oncoming death at the time of her writing it, so her handwriting could've been quite ineligible. That, and when writing something up one can often assume what a word is by looking at it but not fully reading it, and so transcribing it wrong.

However, it was no secret that Barrie did not get on well with Mary, so it 'being nice' for her to have him around was an overstatement if not an outright lie.

It's more likely that Barrie was only able to see himself as being the best person for the boys to be left with, even if it was against their own mother's wishes, and felt desperately protective of them. Conclusively, Jenny never came to fulfil this wish of Sylvia's, if it was her that was indeed wanted.

Sylvia had at least made it abundantly clear to her mother that she wanted her sons to stay together and not be split up and sent off to various different relatives. Despite the extensive family that were willing to help – physically as well as financially – dividing them up would only have distressed them further.

Ultimately, the boys returned to their home in Campden Hill Square, to be cared for and raised by Mary and Barrie.

Peter had begun his first term at Eton with George, and almost immediately came to experience the taunts of his peers for being 'the real Peter Pan'. Already dealing with so much, he didn't even get to see his popular and successful older brother due to the difference in year groups and schedule: George's presence could've potentially helped provide some comfort.

As a result, Peter understandably started to resent the famous play, eventually merging into a lack of fondness for Barrie. Not quite the disconnected relationship Jack was experiencing, but definitely less of the boyhood love he used to feel; Peter no longer got excited for his Uncle Jimmy's visits to Eton in the way George still did, and must've felt that Barrie was at the root of fault for his being teased. In future years, he went on to say that if he had only been named something – anything – different to Peter:

'...*what miseries would have been spared me.*'[5]

If Barrie was ever aware of how Peter was feeling, he never wrote of it, so we have to assume he was either unaware completely or the idea of one of his boys being teased simply never crossed his mind. He did, after all, see them all as flawless beings, incapable of imperfections with means to be teased.

In March of 1911, Barrie wrote to one of his friends:

> *'I have in a sense a larger family than you now. Five boys whose father died four years ago and now their mother last summer, and I look after them, and it is my main reason for going on. The Llewelyn Davies boys.'*[6]

Being the paternal figure to five children without having to be married must've been the perfect scenario for the small man, though he expressed nothing but remorse and grief for the loss of the boys' parents. Perhaps the idea of being their father was more enjoyable to him than the actual responsibility, since there is so much more to raising children than playing with them and supporting them financially. Peter clearly didn't feel able to confide in him as he once might've or as he probably could to his father, and it was probably the huge success and fame of Barrie that was now laying between them.

Barrie never claimed to be their father, and the boys – even small Nico – never came to call him such. He remained 'Uncle Jimmy'.

And of course, between all this, Barrie had to continue with his writing. For the Easter holidays of 1911, all five boys were sent to stay with Emma du Maurier at Ramsgate so that Barrie could continue with writing the novel adaptation of *Peter Pan*, which he was getting close to finishing by this time.

Finally, Hodder and Stoughton released *Peter and Wendy* for the first time as a prose novel. The first editions contained thirteen plates that were illustrated by Francis Donkin Bedford, a British artist who also lived in London.

Peter and Wendy was the original name that Barrie had wanted to name the stage play, and it's interesting to note how he pushed for this again when the novel adaptation was requested by his publishers, which was successful. Making Wendy's character more prevalent in the story is a key theme often overlooked by readers because they are so taken by the magic of Peter and Neverland, which is a shame when Barrie himself clearly admired her.

Wendy was the embodiment of his own mother after all, her childhood days captured in the spirit of a young girl whose name would soon populate British culture.

They are the eyes a mother leaves behind to guard her children

Putting Wendy's name in the title was also Barrie's nudge to children that would come to read the book that they should not want to be like Peter, but like Wendy. Peter was, after all, based off Barrie's biggest self-visualised flaws, and his inability to grow up left him ostracised from his peers throughout his life. Wendy, on the other hand, was written as a mature, intelligent, kind and graceful girl, who grows up precisely when she is meant to while still carrying her belief in Peter, Neverland, and most of all magic, well into adulthood:

> *'Wendy was grown up. You need not be sorry for her. She was one of the kind that likes to grow up. In the end she grew up of her own free will a day quicker than other girls.'* [7]

Wendy's name has been dropped from most Peter Pan adaptations since then, save for the most recently released *Peter Pan and Wendy* Disney live-action remake (2023).

As Peter and Wendy hit the shelves and Barrie's wealth and fame once again rapidly shot up, so did the hype from children around the story of a boy who could fly. Barrie received letters every day from young fans – older ones too – asking about Peter Pan and Tinker Bell and the dastardly Captain Hook. Many parents tried to push their children onto the writer in the hopes he would 'adopt' them in the same way he had done with the Llewelyn Davies boys, but he disliked this behaviour and kept his circle small.

He was recognised every time he ventured into Kensington Gardens and the invitations to parties and dinners rolled in, but Barrie remained as quiet, contemplative, and reserved as ever.

All the while, his five adopted sons were doing considerably well in school in terms of grades and work, and Barrie wanted to make sure that they continued to do well in themselves by arranging for a house in the summer where he would holiday with them.

In a letter to the Duchess of Sutherland, he laid out what he believed was needed for the boys:

> *'...what they yearn for is to be remote from Man and plenty of burn trout fishing, of which they never tire from the rising to the setting of the sun.'* [8]

He also went on to say that money wasn't an obstacle, a comment very much in the nature of Barrie to make.

Subsequently, he came to rent Scourie Lodge for seven weeks across August and September, a Scottish coastal manor house that was largely secluded from the rest of the world.

Jack, however, was not to join them. According to Barrie in a letter to Nurse Loosemore, who he still kept in occasional touch with:

> *'Jack of course is not with us as he is still on his cruise in Canadian waters. But he writes very interesting letters and seems to be very well.'*

He then went on to say:

> *'They are all happy, I think. It is already a year since their mother died.'*[9]

Considering Jack's later statements about his schooling, it's clear that Barrie really didn't seem to have any idea how the boys were actually doing underneath everything, despite his best efforts. There were evident struggles going on with all five, and no amount of Barrie's money or lavish holidays were going to heal them.

In fact, some concern was raised among the family about Barrie's showering of wealth over the boys. Dolly Ponsonby came to say of the matter:

> *'But in his desire to make up to the boys for all they have lost, he gives them every material pleasure. Nothing is denied them in the way of amusement, clothes, toys, etc. It is very, very disheartening, & when one thinks of Arthur, their father – almost unbearable... J.M.B. takes the boys to very grand restaurants in their best evening clothes & they go on to stalls or box at the theatre.'*[10]

Clearly, the general thought was that Arthur had been a hard-working man that didn't earn all that much money in comparison to some of his peers and family, yet he and Sylvia were extremely happy as they were. They were

They are the eyes a mother leaves behind to guard her children

not poor, but they were not rich, either. And in this respect, Arthur aimed to raise his sons to be modest and polite and kind, with the ideology that happiness didn't always come from huge financial success.

Uncle Jim, with his seemingly endless riches, wasn't continuing Arthur's legacy in this fashion at all.

Realistically, Barrie probably believed that keeping them so occupied was the best way to keep them happy after all they'd been through. The holidays, five-star restaurants and theatre trips were a distraction from an inevitable depression that any child would have to deal with amidst their grief, and Barrie wasn't giving them the chance to indulge in sadness.

Otherwise, maybe he thought the boys would love him more if he showered them with the gifts and experiences their parents could not afford. He wasn't their new father and there was nothing he could do to provide that comfort, but he could provide something completely new that came out of the tragedy: riches.

After a summer of fishing and frolicking the high Scottish coast, another school term began and Nico joined Michael at Wilkinson's. For a time, life became rather monotonous and regular for them all.

Michael and Nico began bringing their friends back to the house after the school hours had ended, and these friends often encountered Barrie; most of them expressed a general dislike towards him due to his countenance. Being a withdrawn and quiet man was a fascinating trait of Barrie's when he was around other adults, since they considered this to be his artistic process and probably found it amusing on the whole. Around adolescents, however, they were still young and learning how to be people within their society, and this behaviour came across as unnerving and probably a little intimidating, too.

One of Michael's friends said of being in his presence:

'I was terrified, and didn't dare speak in his presence. He never said a word, just sat like a tombstone. I viewed him with the utmost dislike, and I think that went for most of Michael's friends, though they would never have told Michael.'[11]

Michael still favoured Barrie and was used to him being that way, so wouldn't accept criticism of him. Having known him all his life, he wouldn't consider his behaviour as anything strange, just typical of his Uncle Jimmy.

And at this point, Barrie was in a position of having to watch his favourite adopted son growing up and finding his place amid his own peers, friends that were taking Michael away from him and the stories he'd been telling him all his life. It's a process that all parents must go through, to let their children go, but for Barrie – who had always struggled with his own growing up – was now struggling with that of the boys he'd come to see as his own.

In the spring of 1912, the Peter Pan statue was secretly erected in Kensington Gardens on the night of 30th April, after lock-out time. It gave the impression to those first May morning wanderers of the gardens that it had appeared by magic overnight, sticking to the general aura of the story.

But this wasn't quite the overall reaction that was expressed by the public: Barrie's audacity to publicise his work in such a huge way was questioned, along with the actual right he was or wasn't given to go ahead with it. The writer had hoped to incite wonder but instead received baffled confusion, which was only mirrored upon himself when he actually saw the statue for the first time.

Overall, Barrie wasn't satisfied with the end product. He'd provided photographs of Michael to the sculptor for reference, since that was the character's main inspiration, but Frampton had used another boy as the model instead. When Barrie came to inspect the finished statue, he complained that it didn't 'show the Devil in Peter'.

This is such a key quote made by the author, as this is what is often left out of adaptations to this day. Many future writers, producers and directors would come to interpret Peter's traits to general childish mischievousness when really, the 'Devil in Peter' was that real streak of mean, a genuine lack of compassion that would lead to literal bloodshed. It's a key example of Barrie's Peter being messed with, changed to fit the view of others rather than what it was originally intended to be.

Ultimately, the statue remained, and still stands in Kensington Gardens to this day. Although it really doesn't show much of the Peter that Barrie originally portrayed in his story, it still provides the whimsical sense of Neverland and the imagination of children that brings it to life.

⁌❦⁍

The Llewelyn Davies boys continued on in their studies and George in particular was excelling at school; he hit the local newspapers due

> They are the eyes a mother leaves behind to guard her children

to an excellent catch in a game of cricket that was considered a marvel. Meanwhile, Michael was also doing especially well and made captain of the football team at his school.

Barrie was immensely proud, and as a reward rented an entire castle for the summer of 1912: Amhuinnsuidhe Castle. It was another occasion where the writer was perhaps flaunting his wealth a bit, but unknowingly so; realising that the boys were quickly growing, he wanted to make the most of their youth for as long and as much as possible. He noted in his later dedication to *Peter Pan*:

> '...when one by one you came out of your belief in fairies and lowered on me as the deceiver.'[12]

Barrie's attachment to the boys – particularly Michael – started to reach its peak on this particular trip. He seemed lenient to let Michael out of his sight at all, to the point where he would be screaming out for the boy if he wasn't within reach. Michael, now twelve years old, wasn't completely incapable and had three older brothers that would also have been keeping an eye on him. Nico later said how:

> '...Uncle Jim turned round and found Michael had disappeared – he'd probably wandered off to fish somewhere else. And then we heard the haunting, banshee wail, "Mi-i-ichael-l-l!" It was an extraordinary sound as it echoed through the hills. And of course Michael was always perfectly all right, and wondered what all the fuss was about.'[13]

With the various guests coming and going throughout the holiday, Michael was very apparently the only one that Barrie seemed to have a constant reign on, which would be suffocating for anyone. At one point, George was spending a lot of time with visitor Betty Hawkins, a girl George's own age, and Barrie did not even seem to notice. Peter later wrote of their flirtations:

> 'They enjoyed themselves quite a lot, sheltering from the eternal rain in the fishing-huts by the side of those lonely romantic lochs... On these occasions George forcibly taught me the elements of tact, i.e. the necessity of making myself

scare, and I envied from afar... But I don't think [Barrie] knew what was afoot between George and Betty: not that it amounted to anything.'[14]

This lack of perseverance over George only spotlights the obsession he had with knowing where Michael was constantly, and it was most likely this overbearing nature that inevitably caused Michael to start pulling away from his Uncle Jimmy.

What made Barrie so clingy towards Michael isn't the easiest aspect of the novelist to analyse, but the best conclusion is that Michael was the gateway to the world and wonder of Peter Pan and furthermore back to Barrie's own childhood – and it was slipping away. Growing up could not be avoided, and even though it had been for the fictional boy Barrie had created, all rules still applied to the boy who was the inspiration.

Chapter 11

Stars are beautiful, but they may not take part in anything, they must just look on forever
1912–1914

In April 1913, Michael moved into his accommodation at Eton. Although George had now left the school and started studying at the University of Cambridge in the constituent Trinity College, Michael probably felt a little in his popular older brother's shadow.

And he did not thrive as George did, either; according to some sources he cried himself to sleep most nights and wasn't as sociable with his peers as the rest of them were. Barrie was aware of this, and wrote in a letter to Charles Turley Smith:

> '[Michael] is very lonely there at present, and I am foolishly taken up about it. It rather broke me up seeing him crying and trying to whistle at the same time.'[1]

It seemed that the tumultuous events of the previous three years had finally caught up with the young boy, and as an instinctive response he wanted his mother. Further from that, he could never call upon her again. It was at this time that Michael probably began to develop a depression that he never really came back from, which has since led to lots of speculation around the events to come.

Barrie wrote that no one seemed to suffer from losing a mother as much as Michael did.

Since he was boarding at Eton, Michael now had no distraction in the form of his Uncle Jimmy at the end of the school day. No games, no stories and no guardian to turn to. No Mary Hodgson either, to provide the maternal care that he still would've needed at such a tender age. He felt such a deep loneliness that it led him to request for Barrie to write to him every single day – upon the Scotsman's offer.

Michael wrote replies to these letters every day as well, so that across his years at Eton there were approximately 2000 letters shared between them. These letters never reached the eyes of anyone outside of the family, as Peter Llewelyn Davies had them destroyed in 1952, saying that they were 'too much'.

This phrasing from Peter ignited the suggestion that the letters contained some inappropriate communications between Barrie and Michael. Rumours regarding Barrie's sexuality and relationship to the boys stemmed from this, and the suggestion that he was abusive to Michael in a sexual and emotional way became a very automatic route that people have been going down for years, especially since the uncovering of Jimmy Savile's horrific past with children. The lack of evidence, however, puts this assumption into redundancy.

In the viewpoint of this book, I believe that Barrie and Michael were merely expressing a paternal and child love for each other, which in that time was not well expressed; men were expected not to express deep emotions such as love between each other. To feel saddened or grieved was also a repressed emotion, even when dealing with major life traumas. The term 'boys don't cry' is a harmful one that is still being deconstructed by society in the modern age, and in Edwardian times was strictly lived by.

As Barrie wrote in his play *Dear Brutus*:

> *'The awful thing about a son is that never, never – at least, from the day he goes to school – can you tell him that you rather like him. By the time he is ten you can't even take him on your knee.'* [2]

However, without the existence of these letters, no theory can be officially proved, only explored. All we have now is Peter's words regarding them who, at the time of him destroying them, was extremely depressed and dealing with the repercussions of being associated with *Peter Pan*.

In June 1913, Barrie accepted a baronetcy – four years after rejecting a knighthood. Now known as Sir James Barrie, his status in society was particularly high for someone who wrote books and plays. It's a wonder that Barrie never truly lost his humble nature what with his mass of success derived from his writing; indulging in his riches didn't make him bad, especially when he often did it for his five adopted sons. It's likely that he never forgot his roots and the class he grew up in, and this kept him grounded.

From *A Window in Thrums*:

> 'But the poor have fine feelings beneath the grime, as you will discover if you care to look for them...'[3]

The following month, George turned twenty whilst studying at Cambridge, where he'd joined the dramatist club, following in the same footsteps of multiple family members on his mother's side. He brought out his talents on the stage and received praise for his performances, only adding to his array of talents; truly, he was becoming an admirable reflection of his father, certainly doing both his parents proud.

As the eldest and first boy to come of age, however, George also became responsible for his mother's estate, and had to sign a number of documents which, according to Barrie, he found quite upsetting, and became relatively stressed about the responsibility. This is very understandable since he was holding the weight of his family on his shoulders already, having been robbed of the guidance his parents would've offered him upon taking over the family had they lived.

Barrie did his best to comfort George in a letter he sent to him that November:

> 'Many things besides this will remind you now of the last days at Ashton, and they will take on a new meaning to you... [your mother] did not wish any of you to go to the funeral. It can only be afterwards that a boy realises the unselfishness of a mother's love. It is a pain as well as a glory to him.'[4]

Such words may have been more saddening to read rather than comforting, since remembering the occasion of her death would've been painful. Talking of her wishes that weren't fulfilled due to the lost will was also perhaps a harsh topic to bring up, and it might've been better to mention better memories of Sylvia from when she was alive and well.

It's as if Barrie were venting his own grief for his own mother onto pages that George would read, rather than genuinely considering that this was another person, with a different mother. Once again, this is an act that can be attributed to childish immaturity and unintentional selfishness, in which Barrie was not aware that he might be upsetting the person at the other end of the conversation.

> *'...and thus it will go on, so long as children are gay and innocent and heartless.'*[5]

Christmas 1913 saw the ninth year of *Peter Pan* running at the theatre, and it was to be the last year that Pauline Chase would play Peter; just as Peter Pan would kill off the Lost Boys that were getting too old, the production team had to cut the cast members that were starting to look too aged to play their child roles.

Pauline Chase wrote of this annual event in *Peter Pan's Postbag*:

> *'Measuring day is one of the many tragedies of Peter Pan.'*[6]

The very literal occasion of 'measuring day' that had to take place before the rehearsals could start is quite a morbid concept. Each cast member was physically measured in comparison to their costume as well as inspected for signs of age, and if they didn't pass inspection then they were removed from the play there and then.

It was no doubt a sad occasion when the cast – who had all bonded through their experiences of performing the groundbreaking play – would unexpectedly have to say goodbye to those that wouldn't be returning for that year's run, which in itself is a reflection of one of the lost themes in the book. In *Peter and Wendy*, the Lost Boys each have their own tree they use to enter the Underground Home, which is fitted to them exactly, and they aren't allowed by Peter to outgrow them because that means they're growing up. Slightly knows he is growing and makes adjustments to his tree without Peter knowing, because otherwise Peter would exile him in the manner befitting his mood – it could be banishment, or it could be death.

Barrie was always present at the rehearsals for each season. In the most recent years, Michael had started to accompany him and offer his opinion which was extremely valued by his adoptive father. Holding the young boy on this pedestal was likely another unintentional damaging factor on him; Barrie possibly thought it would make him feel important and wanted, whereas Michael would interpret it all as never being able to amount to all that his Uncle Jimmy had achieved in life.

The months ending 1913 and the beginning of 1914 saw Barrie caught up in another flirtation with actress Gaby Deslys, who was reportedly not particularly good at her art but a great hit with audiences due to her flamboyance; her seductive manner and dress was what brought her fame and popularity, and Barrie was determined to write her into his next play.

He was swept up into the new technology of cinematography at this time, fascinated so much by it that he set out to make his next project to incorporate the new form. He planned to write a play – with Gaby as the star – where previously-filmed scenes would be projected onto the back of the stage behind the performance.

Barrie's old friend, Charles Frohman, visited during the Easter period to hear Barrie's new ideas, and was initially very skeptical about the incorporation of cinematography and theatre. However, with the success that *Peter Pan* was, he wasn't in a position to turn the writer down due to uncertainty. Subsequently, he suggested a trip to Paris to discuss further development.

Barrie brought George, Peter and Michael along for the trip, to which Peter recalled a string of pomposity and grandiosity, going in and out of cafés and restaurants and even a well-known red-light district.

> 'George took to all of this like a duck in water... and it was then that George and I first clearly saw what Jack had missed by being sent into the Navy instead of to Eton.'[7]

The boys were becoming more and more self-aware of their situation as they got older, and despite Barrie's best intentions for them, they were all pawns in a game of grown-ups, caught up in a world where exposure was thrust upon them far too early. The fame of a play, a writer and a story had put them into a world of publicity whether they wanted it or not, and as long as they had their names, there was no escape from the association.

In the summer, Barrie kept up tradition and took the boys to Scotland for the summer holidays for fishing – apart from Jack, who was with his ship in the North Atlantic as a Sub-Lieutenant. As Peter had now started to notice, the consistency of Jack's absence on these holidays leaves little wonder of how he came to feel so distant from Barrie, the man who he was supposed to know as 'Uncle Jim'. He was missing out on all the fun his brothers got to partake in, and realistically barely knew who they were all growing up to be. Being separated from siblings is hard enough, especially when there are multiple that get to stay together, so Jack's complete isolation from them wasn't helped by the fact that four of them still got to spend regular time together whilst he'd been quite literally cast out to sea.

It was during this summer trip to Scotland that Barrie was starting to catch wind of the murmurs of war. In a letter to Lord Lucas, he wrote:

> *'We are so isolated from news here, that when I wrote last I was quite ignorant that Europe was in a blaze... We occasionally get the morning paper in the evening, and there may be big news to-day.'* [8]

On 4th August 1914, Britain declared war on Germany. James Barrie and the Llewelyn Davies boys fished blissfully unaware until Peter's late arrival to the holiday on 6th August, bringing the terrible news along with a letter for George.

> *'The letter proved to be a circular from the Adjutant of the Cambridge O.T.C., pointing out that it was the obvious duty of all undergraduates to offer their services forthwith...'* [9]

George, being over eighteen, was expected to join the ranks and serve Britain in the Great War. Peter was also on the cusp of being of age and could be considered for drafting since he'd left Eton and was due to join his brother at Trinity College the following term.

Conclusively, George and Peter travelled down to London that evening with the intention of getting themselves commissioned. Despite the determination, the two of them must've felt extremely anxious; the news of war and expectation to fight in it had landed upon them so suddenly, especially when just days before George had been happily fishing his time away in the highlands. Now, he was on a train with dozens of other young men looking to join the cause, younger brother at his side.

Peter later came to write of the occasion:

Stars are beautiful, but they may not take part in anything

> '...I think George as well as I had odd sensations in the pit of the stomach as we emerged from Winchester Station and climbed the hill to the Depôt. At any rate George had one of those queer turns, something between a fainting fit and a sick headache, to which he had been prone since childhood, and had to sit for a few minutes on a seat outside the barracks. I would willingly have turned tail and gone back to London humiliated but free. George however, the moment he recovered, marched me in with him through those dark portals...'[10]

The Lieutenant Colonel who saw the boys that day – J.R. Brownlow – was quick to hand them the relevant forms to sign. He informed them that upon sending the signed forms back they'd be able to pick up their uniforms and find their names amongst the hundreds of others in the paper.

Just like that, George and Peter found themselves with the King's commission to serve in the Special Reserve of the 60th Rifles.

Barrie was now fifty-four years of age and deemed too old to serve in the war: the cut-off age was forty-one. He didn't let this stop him and wished to do whatever he could to help with the effort, and started by offering financial aid to Lord Lucas for his family home-turned hospital. His large donation was accepted gratefully.

Additionally, towards the end of August, Barrie received an indirect summons from Prime Minister Asquith to write a propaganda play that would highly praise the cause of the allies. This ultimately meant putting aside all plans he had for his play with incorporated motion picture, casting aside Gaby Deslys for the honourable task. Several other prestigious authors were approached to write similar propaganda pieces as well, including H.G. Wells.

With not much else he could realistically do, Barrie agreed to write a play of these requirements to the best of his ability.

> 'It all goes to show that the war will be a long one... Nothing in men's minds & faces here but the seriousness of the war...'[11]

The Dark Side of Peter Pan

As Barrie worked away back in London, George and Peter returned to Scotland where Michael and Nico had remained with Mary Hodgson to await their summons, making the most of the fishing whilst they still could.

George spent a lot of his time writing to a young woman he'd met back in 1912, when he and his brothers had made friends with her and her sisters at a dance hosted by Sylvia's sister. Josephine Mitchell-Innes had captured his attention, so the pair were now engaged. It was in these letters that George must have vented most of his anxiety about the war because Josephine's sister Norma later came to say:

> '...George had absolutely no illusions whatsoever. He knew what he was in for from the word go.'[12]

George was intelligent enough not to see the war as an opportunity to play soldier, which is a melancholy retrospective in the events that were to play out.

On 9th September, the anxiously awaited letter for George and Peter arrived: their orders to report to Sheerness for training.

All this time, Jack was still on his ship in the North Atlantic, and according to Barrie, wasn't allowed to reveal much about anything – not his location, activities or even his daily movements about the ship – no doubt due to the nature of confidentiality in warfare. Barrie did his best to keep the second of the Llewelyn Davies boys in the loop with what was happening with his brothers, but Jack was likely feeling so detached from them at this point that he didn't feel the same effect as the others might have upon the news of George and Peter going off to fight.

As the weeks went on, Barrie became increasingly frustrated with his lack of assistance towards the war effort. With three of his boys now involved with the war effort, he had no control of what was to happen to them no matter how worried for their safety he may be, and with them all growing older, more independent and needing him less, he was feeling decidedly useless.

Eventually, on impulse, he decided to put himself to any kind of use he could think of, and decided to travel over to America in an attempt to raise support for the allies. He boarded the RMS *Lusitania*, which was fated to sink the following year after being torpedoed by a German U-Boat.

Stars are beautiful, but they may not take part in anything

Barrie's initial plans were soon thwarted. When his ship docked in New York, he was met by a stern warning from the Consul-General and the British Ambassador not to go through with his initial plans for the trip, due to a concern of possibly offending anyone. As a result, he took to shutting himself up in the Plaza Hotel with the intention of avoiding all media press, who had caught wind of his arrival and were ecstatic about catching an interview with him.

The plan to remain isolated only worked for so long. A reporter from the *New York Herald* somehow managed to break into Barrie's suite at the hotel and, without first being detained by any security, scored an interview with the famous writer.

It was this interview, incidentally, that Barrie would succeed in a different area: keeping hope. He spent most of the interview talking about children, particularly the ones he favoured most. He spoke of how the Llewelyn Davies boys had inspired the character of Peter Pan as well as Neverland and all the magical things that lived and happened there – how two of those boys were now off fighting in the Great War.

It was this interview that seemed to revive *Peter Pan* in a new sense, re-igniting the world's love for the story, because it showed that even in a war that had enraptured the world, innocence could still and had to be protected. Boys as young as fourteen were being drafted into the army despite the minimum age being eighteen, and a whole generation of children would be affected in the years to come. But the island of Neverland and the adventures that could happen there created a distraction.

It is perhaps this very element of Peter Pan that people always hold on to in times of darkness, when stories of good defeating evil and children being triumphant in their adventures are enough to obscure all the terrible things in the world.

> *"'You just think lovely wonderful thoughts… and they lift you up in the air.'"* [13]

Chapter 12

Peter was not quite like other boys; but he was afraid at last 1914–1915

Arriving at Sheerness for their training, George and Peter were met with the hustle and bustle of things already progressing quickly; other young soldiers who'd arrived only the previous week were being sent to the front due to the heavy amount of casualties there had already been since the breakout of war.

Peter later set the scene of the boys and men he met upon their arrival:

> 'Average age about twenty-one; on the whole a devoted, laughing, fatalistic, take-it-as-it-comes company, often coarse of tongue, too young to be coarsened of body or soul by the asperities of adult life – the bloom of youth on them still...'[1]

This depiction is just one young man's alone, there would come to be thousands more, and it's already a raw insight of the generation's youth – all their bright flames so quickly extinguished. The very life of people at the time and they were being sent to fight in a war that would wipe out a majority.

Barrie was clearly concerned for the boys and their engagement in the war. By this time, he would be seeing the consistency of negative headlines as well as hearing the general conversation about it all in society. He wrote a letter to George in November 1914:

> 'I enclose you the Eton Chronicle, from which I see that 8 percent of Etonians have been killed. In the army all over the percentage of killed is under 2 per cent...'[2]

Peter was not quite like other boys; but he was afraid at last

These were probably not facts he should've been sharing with a young man facing this potential fate, since George's anxiety at the impending war would have only increased, and he wasn't in a position to back out of joining due to the consequences of 'deserting'.

(The penalty for desertion – absconding without official permission for leave – was execution.)

However, Barrie did admit in a later letter:

> *'What you don't know in the least is the help you have been to me and become more and far more as these years have passed. There is nothing I would not confide in you or trust to you.'*[3]

This suggests that the main reason why Barrie came across as inappropriate to the boys is because he saw them all as his friends still. When he first met them in Kensington Gardens, he'd play with them and interact with them as if they were fellow peers, and the transition to them being his adopted sons left some blurred lines.

George was posted to the 4th Battalion of the Rifle Brigade in December, in preparation for his march to the front. He was allowed a short leave before his shipment in which Barrie hosted him at his London flat only too keenly. Whether he wanted to provide a good distraction from the coming days or to give one last extravagance to one of his favourites, Barrie made plans to entertain him with a few hours visiting Gaby Deslys.

She was still on the side of Barrie's projects as his propaganda play was the forefront of his attention. It was called *Der Tag*, meaning the German toast for victory, and when it was staged many saw it as taking favour with the Germans too much – it's safe to say it wasn't too successful.

The time for George to leave came and Barrie had to say goodbye. Peter was to remain at Sheerness whilst his brother was off to the front, which must've been a difficult separation after their close few weeks together.

Barrie's personal notes from this time makes it adamant how he was feeling about George's departure, as well how the other boys were gradually moving away from him and progressing in their own lives, independent from their guardian. Barrie wrote of a new idea, one of a frequent many he would take note of:

> ' *–The Last Cricket Match. One or two days before war declared – my anxiety and premonition – boys gaily playing cricket at Auch, seen from my window – I know they are to suffer – I see them dropping out one by one, fewer & fewer.*'[4]

He managed not to show his distress from fear of losing the boys around them somehow, other than the odd hint in his letters to George, of course. In hindsight, it's a cruel irony that his fears and premonitions would slowly come to be a reality, the tragedy of all the loss Barrie dealt with in his life. It's because of this reason that he seemed to always expect the worst, as if he saw himself as a bad omen that would poison those he loved around him. In the end, he would be a man left alone.

As George prepared for departure in the midst of the Christmas season, the most interesting item he packed into his kit bag was a book that he'd purchased for himself just a few days before. This book was *The Little White Bird*.

Why he decided to take this particular book with him – and go out of his way to buy a copy specifically for his travels – is quite a sentimental and touching notion. It also proves something that many ignore: there was definitely love for his Uncle Jimmy. Despite what other speculations have been made since about the nature of their relationship, if George truly felt any resentment towards the man, the likelihood of him taking a book Barrie had written – especially one that so directly related to the childhood George experienced with him – is extremely low. And the story that re-gripped the nation in such uncertain times and provided comfort was clearly having a similar effect on George.

Despite the outbreak of war, *Peter Pan* showed again at the theatre that Christmas for its tenth year. In a sense, it seems a stubborn stand in the spirit of the popular British meme to 'Keep Calm and Carry On'. Ultimately, it was resilience in the face of brutality, a way of keeping hope and childhood innocence alive. With Pauline Chase now out of the cast, Madge Titheradge was her replacement as Peter Pan, and the show went on.

Over in France, George was waiting for orders to advance. With so much spare time to just think, many of his thoughts turned to his mortality and

Peter was not quite like other boys; but he was afraid at last

other morbid subjects. He wrote to Peter, who was still training at Sheerness, to ask if he would be the one to let Josephine (his fiancé) know if he was killed, so that she wouldn't have to read of his death in the newspapers first. In response, Peter wrote:

> *'...if I thought the war was bound to last more than a year from now, I believe I should commit suicide.'*[5]

This sentence alone is a cruel foreshadowing, almost fictitious, like a terrible fate spoken into reality. But hearing news of the deaths happening at the front would bring even the most positive-minded people down.

George's schedule soon began to fill up as the fighting progressed, and he was left with little spare time to write to anyone when he was not sleeping. The letters between him and Barrie still remained frequent, however, and in January 1915 he was doing his best to assure Barrie that there was no need to worry:

> *'Don't you get worried about me. I take every precaution I can, & shall do very well. It is an amazing show, & I am unable to look forward more than two or three hours. Also don't get anxious about letters. I'll send them whenever there's a chance, but there are less chances than I expected.'*[6]

Barrie responded:

> *'You should see how I plunge thro' my letter-bag looking for one from you. It is almost too exciting, and I have some bad nights, I can tell you.'*[7]

Barrie's love for George was clearly one of the few strings that the writer was clinging to for his mental health, a rather foreign concept at the time. It's a prime example of how intense it may have come across to some, even when this was a time when young boys and men were not returning home alive, or even at all.

January 1915 was the same month that George's Uncle Guy du Maurier (his mother's brother) headed out to the Western Front. He was a soldier as a profession, and in his letters to his wife he didn't hold back on describing the grim conditions of the trenches and the gore he encountered each day. Coincidentally, he was only four miles down from George.

George wrote to Barrie on the 22nd January:

> 'I don't think there's very much danger to expect, except from sickness, which is always ready in this weather to show its face... But I take every care that can be taken, I can promise you... I suppose Uncle Guy is somewhere about by now. I should like to come across him, but there isn't much chance... I dare bet he won't have much to say for this game. Picturesqueness is distinctly lacking.'[8]

The use of humour in the face of such horror was quite common among soldiers in the midst of war, and George probably did this in his letters to Barrie to give him some comfort. It was a façade for what he was witnessing in reality; whilst George was writing 'there's nothing for you to be anxious about', his Uncle Guy was writing home to his wife about the trenches being filled with dead bodies:

> 'When one is killed they let him lie in the squelching mud and water at the bottom; and when you try and drain or dig you unearth them in an advanced state of decomposition...'[9]

This is just one of the many details Guy du Maurier had to tell of.

At least with Barrie's letters there often came treats, too; as he had done for George when he was at Eton, Barrie sent hampers of food and books out to him in the trenches, in which the contents were often shared with the other young officers. George responded in thanks:

> 'I ask for the devil of a lot, but everything I get here is worth thirty times what it was in the piping times of peace...'[10]

Such everyday novelties were like gold to the soldiers on the Western Front. In another of Barrie's letters, he wrote:

Peter was not quite like other boys; but he was afraid at last

> *'I had hardly finished reading and re-reading [your letter] (quite as if I was a young lady) when there arrives, unexpected, a gent of the name of Peter... and between you and me a d-v-l-shly handsome fellow in my opinion, and I guess in that of any candid person.'*[11]

This may be what people refer to when they accuse Barrie of inappropriate communications with the boys, but if this were a mother talking, it would not be taken the same way; many mothers referred to their sons as being handsome, and yet a father (or in this case, adoptive father-figure) was judged for doing the same.

As the weeks and months went on, George began to open up to Barrie about the horrors of war he was witnessing every day, whilst still trying to assure Barrie that he himself was immune to any harmful fate:

> *'...I've seen violent death within a yard of me. I was quite safe myself, Uncle Jim, as I was right down underneath the parapet... The top of his head was shot off, so he didn't feel it. But it was a dreadful sight.'*[12]

On 11th March, Barrie wrote a letter to George that seems to encompass their relationship and the nature of it perfectly:

> *'...I do seem to be sadder to-day than ever, and more and more wishing that you were a girl of 21 instead of a boy, so that I could say the things to you that are now always in my heart. For four years I have been waiting for you to become 21 & a little more, so that we could get closer & closer to each other, without any words needed.'*[13]

This quote alone speaks for all the other evidence so far suggested: Barrie did not feel a perverse, romantic love for George or any of the other boys, only wished he could express the love he did feel for them and not be ridiculed. If George were a girl, he could dote on him more openly, as a father could with a daughter. But he was a son, and with that came a societal gate that was frowned upon to open.

In the same letter, he informed George that his Uncle Guy had been killed, doing his best to provide some solace on the harm and death going on all around the eldest Llewelyn Davies boy. He concluded:

> *'I have lost all sense I ever had of war being glorious, it is just unspeakably monstrous to me now.'*

Over in France, George received this letter with the news of his Uncle's death and wrote a reply on 14th March. Barrie was not to receive this letter for another three or four days after.

On 15th March 1915, George was with his troupe marching to drive the Germans out of St Eloi, where they stopped to rest and for the Colonel to talk to them all. Sitting on a bank with his fellow officers, a stray bullet was fired without warning and shot through George's head. He died instantly.

Aubrey Tennyson wrote of the incident to Peter:

> *'...he can have felt nothing... they took him back and buried him in a field on the left of the road... and they took a lot of trouble making the grave look nice, & planting it with violets.'*[14]

Chapter 13

Do you believe in fairies?
1915–1917

'...[Barrie] loved George with an exceeding great love.'[1]

Peter later wrote.

Asleep in their beds in the late evening of 15th March, Mary Hodgson and Nico were awoken abruptly by the sound of someone banging continuously on the front door of the house in Campden Hill Square. Nico remembered the night vividly:

> *'Mary got out of bed and went downstairs, while I sat up with ears pricked. Voices soon came up the stairs, but stopped just short of the landing. Then I heard Uncle Jim's voice, an eerie Banshee wail – "Ahh-h-h! They'll all go, Mary – Jack, Peter, Michael – even little Nico – This dreadful war will get them all in the end!" A little later, realising I was awake, he came and sat on my bed for a while. I don't think he spoke, but I knew that George was dead.'*[2]

Peter received the news of George's death via telegram at Sheerness and left for Adelphi Terrace immediately, shaken by the new fact that his oldest brother had followed his mother and father to the afterlife too early. He described the scene he arrived to at Barrie's flat:

> *'The effect on J.M.B. was dire indeed, poor little devil. Oh, miserable Jimmie. Famous, rich, loved by a vast public, but at what a frightful private cost. Shaken to the core... by the death of Arthur; tortured a year or two later by the ordeal of his*

own divorce; then so soon afterwards prostrated, ravaged and utterly undone when Sylvia pursued Arthur to the grave; and after only four and a half years, George; George, whom he had loved with such a deep, strange, complicated, increasing love... '3

The above quote sums up the biggest tragedy of J.M. Barrie's life; remembered for doing great and charitable things and providing an internationally loved story, but suffering so much behind the curtain of his private life. The loss of George was his most difficult loss he'd ever had to deal with so far.

Over the following days, Michael, Jack, and Nico all arrived at Campden Hill Square to comfort each other in their grief. Five was now four, and it had been so long since the five of them had last been together, and now it would never happen again.

Nico remembered watching Jack softly crying as he stared out of the window whilst he himself was just pleased to be seeing his older brothers, and in their uniforms looking so smart. Being only eleven years old, it's an unsurprising reaction that manifested from his grief.

George's final letter to Barrie had also arrived, and after acknowledging the sad news of his Uncle Guy's death, he wrote more assurances that there was no need for Barrie to worry about him – a cruel and tragic irony.

'I take every care of myself that can be decently taken. And if I am going to stop a bullet, why should it be with a vital place?... Keep your heart up, Uncle Jim... Soon the spring will be on us, & the birds nesting right up in the firing line... I wonder what spring will bring for us in this part of the line.' '4

George was not meant to see the future, and yet he kept high hopes for it.

Peter was particularly affected by his brother's death out of the five boys – which is not to undermine the others' grief – having spent the most time with George in the previous few years. What with the collective years at Eton, joining the army together and training to be in battle, they shared a close bond that the threat of death only solidified. Peter spoke of George in later years, describing how he was personally affected by this loss:

Do you believe in fairies?

> '...we were bound together by that ineffable love of brother for brother which one has occasionally read of. On the other hand it is not in the least untrue to say that I have gone on missing him possibly ever since I last saw him, leaning out of the windows as his train steamed away from Sheerness station calling out, "Till our next merry meeting!"'[5]

Peter then went on to admit:

> '...when he died, some essential virtue went out of us as a family.'

This could be a bitter blaming of all that was to come, or perhaps George really was the glue that had been keeping the family in check since Arthur and Sylvia's demise. It's a natural response to see everything as worse when a close relation passes, and it was no different for Peter.

Despite being rapt with grief himself, Barrie's play starring Gaby Deslys – *Rosy Rapture*[6] – premiered just one week after George's death. It was received by an ultimately unimpressed audience. With everything that had happened, it proved too much for Barrie to deal with alone, so he reached out to Charles Frohman for help.

He asked if Frohman could travel to London from the United States with the hopes he might be able to provide some insight into the play's flaws, and assist in getting it off the ground. Frohman quickly responded in the positive, and his ship, the *Lusitania*, set sail on 1st May. In the midst of a war, this wasn't a wise decision, but he was insistent on getting to his friend and providing his expertise.

Then, on 7th May, the *Lusitania* sank off the Irish coast after being torpedoed by German U-Boats. Frohman was reportedly offered a lifeboat due to his first-class status, but he famously denied the offer, saying:

> 'Why fear death? It is the greatest adventure in life.'[7]

This was a near-perfect mimic of the known quote from *Peter Pan*:

> 'To die will be an awfully big adventure.'

Considering that Frohman wanted to be most remembered for 'bringing Peter Pan to the world' it's the most fitting final message he could've chosen to leave with. His body was later found washed up on the shore below the Old Head of Kinsale, and his journey to London was never completed; after being found, he was taken back to America.

Barrie was unsurprisingly devastated at the news of Charles Frohman's death, as he was not only a great partner in theatre but also a great friend. Being so soon after George's death, it was almost as if every aspect of Barrie's life was crumbling piece by piece around him, and all because of war.

In light of this fresh sorrow, Barrie reacted determinedly and threw himself into assistance with the war, taking over much of the responsibilities of Lord Lucas's home-turned-hospital after Lord Lucas himself joined the Flying Corps. He also had the idea to set up an orphanage for the stray children of the French countryside, orphaned and made homeless from the war. He pledged £2000 to the cause and put the idea to Elizabeth Lucas to have the temporary orphanage set up for them. It kept him busy, making it easier to deal with the double bereavement he'd been dealt in the previous few months.

Setting up the orphanage led Barrie to visiting France in the July, getting quite close to the front line – eighteen miles away, where the sound of guns and cannons could be heard. He witnessed the distressing sight of wounded children, traumatised by the destruction around them, and described in a later letter the dogs that would scavenge for corpses in their hunger. It was Barrie's chance to do what he was best at for the war effort: interacting with children.

In a time of great sorrow and suffering, these children were all equally grieved. Some had lost limbs, some had lost families, and all had lost some part of their innocence. Barrie was at least able to bring shreds of their innocence back to them, in a great act of kindness that many do not know of him. His involvement in the First World War was more than most other novelists at the time, and he didn't let his age and physical inabilities stop him from playing some part in the assistance. Simply playing with and telling stories to the children so affected by the war provided great comfort in the confusing aftermath, even just to ease their fear of what might become of them in later years.

Do you believe in fairies?

When he returned to England, Barrie immediately took Michael and Nico to Scotland for their annual fishing holiday. There was no extravagant castle rented for this year, just a string of hotels, but the rich waters of the fishing remained relatively the same.

It was during this trip that Michael was distancing himself from Barrie more and more; perhaps it was the depths of his own grief for George that caused him to retreat into himself, but Barrie came to describe him more as:

'The dark and dour and impenetrable.'

By September, at the age of fourteen, Michael had endured two years at Eton where he was constantly unhappy. Keeping his feelings pushed down, he had become almost completely withdrawn around his peers. One fellow student, Clive Burt, described him as:

'...a cat that walked alone. He was always very reserved – not a seeker after popularity or great friendships, though both were open to him.'[8]

It can be – and has been – considered that the main reason for Michael's reservedness in the all-boys school was because he was questioning his sexuality. Being around other boys all the time, it's thought that Michael was aware that he was finding himself attracted to his fellow sex rather than any girls and women he'd come across in his life. and was afraid of this fact becoming apparent in his behaviour.

Being homosexual – or having any sort of relations with the same sex – at this time was illegal, so being open about it was completely out of the question for basic safety. It explains why Michael mostly kept to himself, not being very expressive around his peers and secluding himself rather than joining in: avoiding suspicion would've been key. Additionally, with his family already being in the spotlight from association with Barrie, he may have been concerned about any extra attention.

There was at least one other student that was experiencing the same fears and worries: Roger Senhouse was a year Michael's senior and later admitted to having a crush on him at the time. Michael never knew this, and Roger went on to have other relationships with men in his adult life, but he described the impact Michael had on him nonetheless as being near on obsessed with him; his schoolwork became lacking and he spent all his time and resources on trying to impress him.

This is a theory that was never officially confirmed with concrete evidence, but it's a theory that continued to generate proof from appearances in the following few years.

That Christmas, *Peter Pan* once again returned to the stage, but the cast had been a majority lost; only Mr Smee, played by George Shelton, remained from the original cast. Unity Moore was now in the lead role as Peter, and the script had suffered some cutting, too.

The entire scene on the lagoon where Peter and Wendy were stranded – in which Peter nearly drowned – was cut due to being deemed insensitive under the circumstances of young boys dying in the war overseas. The famous line being the main reason: 'To die will be an awfully big adventure.'

September 1916 and the war was still dragging on. George's death that had rocked Barrie and the Llewelyn Davies boys so much was buried under the consistent string of destruction and death that the war was regularly and reliably bringing.

To begin with, Lord Lucas had been killed in action – as had his two nephews – and Elizabeth Lucas, who had been running the hospital at Lord Lucas's home, became so unwell from overexertion that the hospital had to close as a result. Both of these events meant that Barrie's attempts to help with the war effort had been cut short only a short way into the war.

Nico, now fourteen, joined Michael at Eton, where it was arranged for him to stay in the same room in the same house as his brother, which must've been considered due to George's death and thus brought Michael some comfort and companionship. Michael appeared to be happier from this, so Barrie's letters reduced to alternate between the two boys.

Nico settled in much quicker than Michael had. He was even described by one of the tutors as 'the heart and soul of the house'.

Peter, meanwhile, was called up to be sent off to the trenches, a path he was conscious that his older brother took and did not return from. After arriving, he witnessed equal horrors like the indescribable conditions of the

Do you believe in fairies?

trenches as well as his friends being killed around him, and his presence at the Battle of the Somme left such an effect on him that he was sent home after two months away. Although not much was recorded by him of what he experienced, it was reported that his return was due to shell shock and a suffering of eczema.

Peter was put up at the house on Campden Hill Square with Mary Hodgson, who took care of him whilst he recovered. The other three boys had spent the Christmas holiday with Barrie at his flat.

It was around this time that Mary wanted to resign as the boys' carer, which came as quite a shock to Barrie. With all that was going on, he clearly felt that this was an odd time for her to quit not just her job but the family she'd promised her past mistress she'd take care of. With Peter's return home, however, she was put off her resignation for the time being.

In March 1917, Jack was docked in Edinburgh for shore-leave when he met Geraldine Gibb. Within his time there, they fell in love and Jack proposed to her, and they became Gerrie and John to one another – Jack preferred his fiancé to call him by his birth name. Being so smitten with her, he wrote to her from the HMS *Octavia* almost as soon as his leave had ended:

> *'I can honestly hardly believe my stupendous luck. Fancy being engaged to you!... Are you happy to know that someday you'll be Mrs John Llewelyn Davies herself? To me it's so wonderful I'm beaten all of a heap!'*

In the same letter he went on to describe and dote on his brothers, as well as his parents, which is a touching sentiment to involve her in his family so eagerly:

> *'Father died when I was 12 & Mother never really got over it. They were wonderful people, I suppose really rather too perfect to go on. But I should so have loved to go to Mother & say, "Here's a daughter for you at last."... She was so lovely herself that it seems a great pity she hadn't a daughter...'* [9]

Unfortunately for him, his decision to propose without any kind of discussion with Barrie – who did not even know of Geraldine's existence in his adopted son's life – did not bode well and left a bitter taste in the Scotsman's mouth.

When Jack visited home in April and told Barrie of his engagement, he also requested that his guardian give some financial assistance for the wedding along with his blessing. In fairness to Barrie, he was still grieving George and could feel the other boys slipping from him. Michael was distancing himself from him and with the recent events in the war, he was feeling downtrodden. Therefore, the compromise he made to Jack was carefully considered.

Jack broke the news to his fiancé in a letter he wrote whilst he was still at Barrie's flat:

> *'...he says that to gain his consent & help we are to wait a year... I think we can do it, don't you?... Cause if we go against him & get married he'll never help us. I know him well enough to be sure of that... Damn all hard-headed and so-called level headed Guardians. No, I don't mean that because he's been so almighty good to us. I'm an ungrateful beast, but it's so infernally hard to wait.'*[10]

Jack's reaction in turn is understandable, considering that his guardian hadn't really had much input in his life. What with being sent off to the Navy at a young age and missing out on so many activities with his brothers, for Barrie to want such an input at this point is quite audacious. On the other hand, perhaps Barrie just wanted a little recognition of his love for Jack, because money would never have been the issue here.

Jack returned to his ship shortly after this visit whilst Michael and Nico started the summer term at Eton. Peter, now deemed well, was thoughtlessly sent back to the Somme.

With the four boys now occupied and the upheaval of the hospital closing having passed, Barrie wanted to visit George's grave. Since the area where his body was buried was still riddled with war, he needed special permission from the War Office in order to make the trip, which he received in June of 1917. Barrie had a military escort for the trip, and although he wrote of the actual journey to France and the mission of finding George's grave, his feelings on this are unrecorded.

Do you believe in fairies?

It's undoubtable that it was a very difficult time for him. George was the first of the five, the first he'd befriended in Kensington Gardens, and the young man – still a boy in Barrie's eyes – had died out of his control. Barrie had vowed to take care of George after both his parents had died and now, once again, he stared down at the patch of earth his adopted son lay under. Another boy that would be stuck at one age forever – this one twenty-two – and a cruel reflection of Barrie's brother David.

Would all his boys not get to grow up? Was this a curse cruelly brought on from his success from *Peter Pan*? And after everything, did he still believe in fairies and magic as he once so strongly did?

Chapter 14

You can have anything in life if you will sacrifice everything else for it
1917–1918

Life would not get less complicated for Barrie as the four remaining Llewelyn Davies boys continued to grow and mature.

After paying his respects at George's grave, Barrie returned to London to move flats; he remained in the same building but relocated to the flat on the top floor. It had a lot more room with a very large open fireplace, and the extra space was considerably more useful for his four adolescent and adult boys.

When the summer of 1917 rolled around, Barrie took Michael and Nico away for the annual fishing trip in Scotland, this time only for two weeks. On their way travelling north, they stopped off in Edinburgh to meet Jack and his new fiancé. Geraldine later recalled of the occasion:

> 'I was – well, yes – nervous, I knew he'd come up to vet me, but I don't think I was in awe of him. My mother was horrified that I should marry someone who was mixed up with Barrie – she said, "I don't trust that man."... we met them at the station, had dinner at the North British Hotel next to the station... It was an extraordinary dinner: I don't think the Bart [Barrie] said a single word throughout the meal – certainly not to me. Michael talked to me – he was very considerate, tried to make me feel relaxed... All the boys made feverish conversation, but the Bart never said anything. Nor did I.'[1]

Barrie had already confirmed that he was nervous for this meeting, probably for the reason of having to let someone into his close circle whether he liked

You can have anything in life if you will sacrifice everything else for it

them or not. His demeanour was no different to when he attended parties with other people of the same social standing and the boys were used to it, but to a young and nervous woman, Geraldine found it unnerving. She had never come across someone like it before and was predominantly unprepared for the interaction – or rather, lack of.

Barrie came away with Michael and Nico for their holiday, where the usual fishing activities commenced. Three weeks later, on 4th September 1917, Jack and Gerrie were married, with the blessing of Barrie behind them. Clearly, the boys' guardian hadn't disliked Gerrie despite his general aura around her.

Since Jack still had his duty to attend to on his ship, he had to leave his new wife in the hands of his Uncle Jimmy. Gerrie went to stay with Barrie in the first few months of marriage while her new husband was away, and she later described what her time living there with the famous writer was like:

> '*I used to sit in a corner of that huge study, as quiet as a mouse. Sometimes Barrie would talk a lot; at other times he'd be wrapped in silence, except for his cough. Most of the time he paced up and down the room, as if I wasn't there, and then suddenly he'd say something... I remember him asking me if I knew how Guy du Maurier had been killed... And Barrie said, "Yes. He was shot. And he wandered about the battlefield for half-an-hour with his stomach hanging out, begging somebody to finish him off." I was quite horrified. Why did he tell me? Was he deliberately trying to shock me? I never told my husband.*'[2]

This is quite an insensitive thing to have said, particularly to someone Barrie hardly knew, therefore no excuses can be made for him here. It is likely that, in his childish manner, he had no verbal filter on this occasion. He might've even thought that saying this would help break the ice between him and his new adopted-daughter-in-law. Whatever the true reasoning, it really wasn't the right thing to say at all, as it gave the impression that he was purposefully trying to upset her and disliked Gerrie on the grounds that she was Jack's wife, and that he wouldn't have liked anyone Jack had married.

Barrie wasn't the only one that Gerrie had to face similar – if not worse – conduct of: Mary Hodgson also demonstrated dislike but on an entirely different level. Since Geraldine was about to become the new mistress of the house in Campden Hill Square, tensions were going to run high. Initially, this may have prompted Mary to stay on with her job for even longer as she wanted to be sure that the house would be left in good hands.

Gerrie recalled her first meeting of Mary to be equally uncomfortable and unforgettable:

> *'...Barrie took me to meet Mary Hodgson at Campden Hill Square. We waited in a room for her, and then she came in and Barrie said, "Mary, this is Gerrie, Jack's wife – " She gave me a paralysing look but didn't say anything, so I tried to be pleasant and said, "Oh, Mary, do look at this something-or-other we've been sent as a wedding present", whereupon she wheeled round and walked out of the room.'*[3]

At this very apparent and rude reaction, Barrie was reported not to have scolded Mary at all, which in turn would've been unsettling to Gerrie. He was probably afraid to clash with Mary any more than they had already over the years, and she already meant so much to the boys. Nevertheless, Geraldine moved into the house to take up the role of Mistress around the Christmas period of 1917, to which Mary's coldness continued towards the new Lady of the House.

As all this was going on, Peter had been caught up in a bit of a scandal while serving. This had started around the September/October period of the year.

Peter was meant to return to London for leave in October but didn't appear at either of the homes on Campden Hill Square or Adelphi Terrace. The obvious worry was that in the throes of war something fatal had happened to him, until Barrie received a letter. Peter informed him that he was staying in Epping Forest with a married woman and her daughter – and that he was having an affair with the married woman.

The woman in question was Vera Willoughby, a professional artist who was originally from Hungary. She was almost twenty-seven years Peter's senior and her daughter was older than him, too.

You can have anything in life if you will sacrifice everything else for it

Barrie was quite shocked to read of the news so bluntly written and it caused a rift between him and Peter. It was, however, something that he and Mary Hodgson agreed upon in their disapproval, which was a rare occurrence. And with Mary still causing a stir with Geraldine, Barrie was intent on staying on good terms with her.

Mary kept her hackles up with her charge's new wife. Gerrie recalled what the dynamic in the house was like:

> *'Mary absolutely refused to speak to me. Everything was communicated via Michael or Nico, or written down as messages on bits of paper... J.M.B. had told me I was in charge, and so I had to try my best... I tried on one or two occasions to be pleasant to Mary, to try and coax her into conversation, but she adamantly refused to address one word to my face. If I was standing next to Michael, she would convey her answers to him, always referring to me in the third person.'*[4]

Such treatment understandably caused Gerrie a lot of stress since she was having to be around it constantly. Sadly, the high tensions in the house were a taboo subject between the family and even Barrie did nothing to try and pacify the situation. Eventually, all the friction finally reached a climax.

In January 1918, Geraldine was alone in the house on a morning that Barrie and the boys had all left early. She came downstairs to find a note from Mary that read:

> *'Either you leave this house or I do.'*

Gerrie recalled her reaction on finding the note:

> *'I started packing there and then, telephoned my husband who had gone to see a friend, he came back to help with some of the luggage, and by night-fall we were staying in a hotel off Knightsbridge.'*[5]

Finally away from the house and Mary's passive aggressiveness, Gerrie was able to calm down from the distress the situation had caused. Unfortunately, she hadn't known she was pregnant and suffered a miscarriage that evening.

After a short stay in respite, it was decided that neither Jack nor his wife would be returning to the house on Campden Hill Square and Mary, after hearing of the consequence of her cruel actions, was so mortified that she handed in her resignation for good. Mary's guilt was so extreme that she refused to accept a leaving sum of money that Sylvia had wished for her to take in her will, along with Barrie's matching addition, which altogether totalled £1000. According to inflation rates, in 2023 that amount equates to just shy of £20,000.

Michael and Nico could not see bad against Mary despite what had happened, and hinted in letters that Jack and Gerrie were partly to blame for things, too. Mary was effectively their receptacle for a mother and had raised them up since birth, and the quickness of the engagement and marriage between Jack and Gerrie may have caused the boys to feel a little resentment at not being told about anything by their brother. Furthermore, Michael tried to convince Mary to take the money that was offered to her upon her resignation, as he wouldn't turn against her even with her hand in the situation.

Overall, the whole affair between Mary and Gerrie and Gerrie's miscarriage was never directly addressed, and although Mary kept contact with the boys after she left, she no longer saw them as often, and also never met any of the other boys' future wives.

With Mary no longer keeping 23 Campden Hill Square running and Geraldine too traumatised to return as mistress, the house was no longer needed; the two youngest boys, Michael and Nico, permanently moved in with Barrie at his flat in Adelphi Terrace. They were of course still living at Eton College during term time, however.

Michael was due to enlist that November, and with that looming, the year passed in the same fashion as always, with Barrie treating the boys at every opportunity possible and keeping them entertained when they visited for the holidays. He was hyper-aware that Michael was getting close to being old enough to join the fighting, George's fate haunting his potential future.

Then, as luck would have it, on 11th November 1918 – the very day before Michael was due to enlist – an armistice with Germany was signed in Compiègne. On 'the eleventh hour of the eleventh day of the eleventh month', a ceasefire came into effect.

You can have anything in life if you will sacrifice everything else for it

    The Great War was over and Michael, initially faced with following a similar route to his oldest brother, was free. Barrie's justified fear of losing the son he saw as his own was now relieved and Michael was supposed to be facing his whole life full of promise and potential ahead of him. After the turmoil of the previous few years, things looked as if they could finally settle for Barrie, with no suspicion to the false sense of security that seeing Michael live brought.

Chapter 15

The moment you doubt whether you can fly, you cease for ever to be able to do it
1918–1921

The end of the First World War had been sudden, slightly unexpected and a complete relief to the people of Great Britain. So many lives had been lost in those four years and Barrie's own relief at all Michael's potential ties with the war being cut is apparent in his letters. George had been devastatingly lost on the battlefield, but Michael at least would be spared, seemingly free from the fate of death.

This relief would not eliminate his anger, however; a lot of the generation's youth had been lost and Barrie, always being so in tune with children and young adults, felt outraged and greatly disappointed on their behalf. For a later speech, he sympathised with them in the notes he wrote:

> *'Old advising young with advice rather a mockery just after War which young men died for...'*[1]

Losing George was obviously the main thought behind this, but even if George hadn't been killed it's likely that Barrie still would've expressed this.

For Peter too, the war had affected him deeply and he returned home a changed person. Many people observed that his spirit was broken from all he had seen and experienced, so even those that had survived the war were now living with a post-traumatic stress that wasn't well understood at the time.

With Michael having dodged being enlisted, he was doing particularly well at Eton: he was in Pop (a society for elite prefects), a co-editor of the

The moment you doubt whether you can fly

Eton College Chronicle as well as a renowned player for the football team, just to name a few of his achievements. After the news of the war ending had broken, he made it clear that he wanted to travel the world now that he was able to. In particular, he expressed a wish to go to Paris just as his grandfather, George du Maurier, had done.

E.V. Lucas wrote of Michael at this time:

> *'He seemed to have everything at his feet, and one used to look at him and wonder what walk of life he would choose; but he gave few signs, being, for all his vivid interest in the moment, more in the world than of it, an elvish spectator rather than a participant.'* [2]

Barrie, being Michael's legal guardian, was not agreeable in letting him go off to Paris, however. He instead implored him to get a degree from Oxford University first, which Michael conceded to. He started his studies in January 1919.

At least at Oxford, Michael was still living independently from Barrie and around other likeminded peers. It gave him the better opportunity to explore his sexuality and express himself more freely, which he may have been learning around this time wasn't too uncommon, especially in a university environment, despite the laws and judgement against it. Even his younger brother, Nico, later confessed to have gone through a similar questioning and experimentation in his life:

> *'...I did go through a more or less bi-sexual stage, I never mentioned it to [Barrie].'* [3]

Michael was joined at Oxford by a fellow pupil from Eton, Roger Senhouse, so he already had a friend when he started there, at least. A new friend he made, Robert Boothby, said of Michael and their friendship group:

> *'I don't think Michael had any girl-friends, but our friendship wasn't homosexual; I believe it was – fleetingly – between him and Senhouse, yet I think Michael would have come out of it.'* [4]

There is no concrete proof of Michael having any homosexual relationship with Roger Senhouse, though his friend's suspicion is validated since they all lived in close quarters with each other.

Having a few good friends meant that Michael was becoming more comfortable around other people, and probably starting to feel a little suffocated by Barrie's affections. It's not uncommon for adolescents to feel this way about their parents when wanting to gain some independence, Michael being no different. Robert Boothby went on to describe what he saw of Michael's relationship with his Uncle Jimmy:

> *'Michael took me back to Barrie's flat a number of times, but I always felt uncomfortable there. There was a morbid atmosphere about it. I remember going there one day and it almost overwhelmed me, and I was glad to get away. We were going back to Oxford in Michael's car, and I said, "It's a relief to get away from that flat", and he said, "Yes it is."... It was an extraordinary relationship between them – an unhealthy relationship. I don't mean homosexual, I mean in a mental sense... it went beyond the bounds of ordinary affection... Michael was very prone to melancholy, and when Barrie was in a dark mood, he tended to pull Michael down with him... when all is said and done, I think Michael and his brothers would have been better off living in poverty than with that odd, morbid little genius.'*[5]

From this statement we can at least confirm that Michael was suffering from depression, as was Barrie, and through their mental illnesses were not good for one another. However, claiming that Michael and his brothers would've been 'better off living in poverty' is a statement that Nico wholly disagreed with:

> *'I am quite unable to admit that J.M.B.'s influence was "unhealthy": oppressive maybe and over-constant – and I can believe that Michael was relieved to get away from the flat, as many many undergraduates have felt as they were speeding from their home with a friend back to Oxford. But so far as I am concerned, speaking as the fifth brother, I'm glad I lived with that odd little man rather than... virtually any other person I have ever known.'*[6]

Considering that Nico was the only other brother that had known Barrie since birth, his account is more reliable than that of Robert Boothby, especially since he entered Michael's life so much later and was only witness to the relationship he had with Barrie for a few short years.

Additionally, Barrie's general demeanour was already extremely odd to the general public and many found him rude and uncomfortable to be around if they weren't used to his ways. This does not equate to him being a bad person, but of the time especially he deviated from the societal norm.

Michael's wish to be away from Barrie – just as Nico suggested – was first and foremost a natural reaction for a young student at university. Once he tasted independency there was no going back. Secondly, we've already explored how Barrie's love for his adopted sons was so great that he struggled to hold in his emotions in the way that grown men were expected to at the time. From the statements examined over the years, they have given the impression that Barrie was manipulative and wanted control; on the contrary, he just wanted to be able to show affection to the boys he saw as his sons and greatest friends. His behaviour was normal for the boys and something they were used to, but as they got older and felt the need to practice independency, it clearly became overbearing as they needed a caregiver less and less.

In a letter written by Nico in 1975, he addressed the speculation around Barrie and the nature of his relationship with the Llewelyn Davies boys:

> *'I haven't the skill to answer about J.M.B. being 'in love' with George and Michael. Roughly, yes – I would agree: he was in love with each of them: as he was in love with my mother: when you come to Mary Ansell it's a different 'feeling'...'*[7]

Michael set off for Paris in July 1919 after finishing his first terms at Oxford. Despite Barrie's resistance, he was determined to get his summer in Paris, and he travelled with three of his fellow students: Robert Boothby recalled how Michael seemed to thrive:

> *'Michael loved Paris: he could speak fluent French, and I think he had a romantic idea of setting up his easel on the left bank and becoming an artist.'*[8]

It's possible that the distance of the channel between him and life back in London was a great help to Michael in feeling detached from English society. He was able to access his true self without risking the judgement of those he knew around him. Plus, it was the grown-up adventure that he needed.

When he returned to England at the end of the summer and continued his studies at Oxford, Michael was reported to be agitated and discontent – he yearned to travel again now that he'd had a taste of it. Perhaps his depression was eased when exploring somewhere new.

All this time, Barrie had been working on a new play: *Mary Rose*. It followed a young mother who disappeared, then reappeared years later but completely unaged. She searched for her son but he was now grown up and she couldn't recognise him. The rehearsals for this began in April 1920.

Michael was not present as he normally was to lend his opinions that were so valued by his Uncle Jim. This was because he had made a new friend at Oxford that he'd become basically inseparable from: Rupert Buxton.

Buxton had been through a considerably tumultuous time before Oxford just as Michael had, so the pair probably bonded over their troubles. Previously, he'd been to Harrow School where he'd been Head Boy, but the war had taken two of his brothers after one was killed while serving and the other contracted pneumonia. Buxton had also lost his father in an accident involving a motorcar and by 1919 his family were suffering financially. Overall, Rupert was known to be quite depressed.

Interestingly, Rupert Buxton was also the topic of a mysterious incident. In December 1918 when he was living at Harrow, he received an unsigned letter advising him to be at a certain place at a specific time that evening. Unsuspecting, he went. He did not return to the house that night. The following day, another letter arrived in the same handwriting to the house at Harrow, explaining vaguely that "his brains were needed". It concluded, "Ill if he refuses, well if he agrees." A telegram signed "Rupert" was then received that night from nearly 300 miles away saying that he would be on the train arriving in London from Newcastle the following evening. He arrived exhausted and received medical care afterward at a London hotel. The incident was reported in *The Times of London* but no account of what really happened was ever published.

The moment you doubt whether you can fly

This could've been a traumatic event that he later confessed the details of to Michael. Otherwise, this is a mystery that was never solved or revealed to the public.

Rupert and Michael met after Rupert transferred from Cambridge to Oxford in the autumn of 1919 and by spring 1920, they were inseparable. The pair went on a hike that took them from Chichester to Beachy Head (around fifty miles) and shared a love of poetry. Rupert was also reported to have been quite liked by Barrie, an accomplishment for any peer that was taking up Michael's time.

Others around the pair didn't seem to approve of the friendship, however, mainly the close friends that Michael already had at Oxford. Robert Boothby claimed:

> '...he had a morbid influence on Michael: he was dark, gloomy, saturnine, with an almost suicidal streak in him. I remember Michael asked me, "Why don't you like my being friends with Rupert Buxton?" And I said, "The answer to that is doom – I have a feeling of doom about him."... when Buxton came along, the gaiety left.'[9]

Some have put down Boothby's comments to jealousy, which does line up with his previous admittance to having a crush on Michael; history would also come to support the accusation.

As Michael and Rupert became closer and more attached, the relationship between Michael and Barrie seemed to weaken. Macktail wrote:

> 'Barrie tried not to see it, and was wretched and miserable when he did... He needed this boy's love also, more than anything on earth...'[10]

In the summer of 1920, Michael came to a conclusion and resolved to make his own decisions – without any input from his Uncle Jimmy. He chose to leave Oxford University and attend the University of Paris, starting in the autumn term.

Barrie's reaction to this is unknown but he proceeded to rent out an entire island off the Scottish coast for August and September that summer, a response that speaks volumes. Perhaps he was thinking of ways to convince Michael to stay or even prove to him just how much he loved him by showering him with examples of his wealth. It was also potentially an opportunity to remind Michael how fun he could be; he let Nico and he invite some friends along for the holiday.

The rest of the party included Roger Senhouse, two of Nico's friends from Eton and Elizabeth and Audrey Lucas. Any adolescent would be grateful and excited for the chance to bring their friends along on holiday and although Barrie had been the one to suggest and allow it, he soon came to regret it.

He wrote to his secretary, Cynthia Asquith, about how left out he was feeling on 17th August, claiming that they were all having a lot more fun without him. Expressing his feelings in this sulking manner reflects that of a child whose friends wouldn't wait for him to catch up, yet Barrie was now sixty years of age.

It was during this holiday that Michael suddenly decided not to go to Paris after all and return to Oxford – the reasoning for this change of heart is unrecorded but it was in line for what Barrie wanted, so it's likely that his plans to win Michael over during that holiday were successful. That, or perhaps Barrie's sulking made Michael feel too guilty to leave him.

Michael spent Christmas in Paris instead, but with Barrie and Nico instead of his friends, and ultimately saw himself back at Oxford in the new year of 1921.

During the school year, Barrie occupied his time with working on a new play called *Shall We Join the Ladies?*[11], a murder play he'd written for Michael. It was under Michael's supervision throughout the writing process but the rehearsals were having to make do without him. The huge cast, with multiple big names and actors that Barrie had previously worked with, included the likes of Fay Compton, Madge Titheradge and Gerald du Maurier just to name a few. *Peter Pan* had also just had its sixteenth revival on stage which Barrie was always making notes on; adding things in, taking them away and altering the script. It was for this revival that Barrie added in the fact that Captain Hook had previously been a British MP as well as an alcoholic before his story in Neverland began, something rarely known by fans.

Barrie did see Michael briefly over the Easter holidays in Dorset, where the adolescent was staying with Rupert Buxton to prepare for their summer exams. The two friends had been staying there alone before Barrie joined them.

The fact that they were staying together alone raises a number of questions considering the previous suspicions to the nature of their relationship, all of which come back to Michael's sexuality. It's possible that this holiday solidified in Michael's mind that what he felt for Rupert wasn't platonic but romantic, and the likelihood of them being able to share a life together was non-existent. Furthermore, it could be suggested that it was during this time the two boys came to a pact, a decision that would take them off the board completely.

Barrie appeared oblivious to any of Michael's activities at this stage.

Interestingly, Barrie started writing a play in 1917 that well encompassed his pent-up emotions towards Michael, called *The New Word*.[12] It followed a father and son who felt unable to audibly communicate their fondness for one another due to sheer embarrassment.

> '*MR TORRENCE. ...My boy, be ready. I hate to hit you without warning. I'm going to cast a grenade into the middle of you. It's this, I'm fond of you, my boy.*
>
> *ROGER (squirming). Father, if any one were to hear you!*
>
> *MR TORRENCE. They won't. The door is shut, Amy is gone to bed, and all is quiet in our street. Won't you – won't you say something civil to me in return, Roger?*
>
> *...*
>
> *I dare say your mother would beam if you called me 'dear father'...*
>
> *ROGER. I don't think so... It's so effeminate.*

These lines in particular are so prominent in what they represent: Barrie wanted so desperately to just openly love the boys as the sons he'd always wanted, but etiquette of the time just did not understand such affection between men. When it came to George, Barrie felt like he never got to convey his love for him. With Michael, who was now at university and with close friends that he was excelling around, the chance was slipping.

And then it was gone.

On 19th May 1921, Barrie was confronted at the entrance to the building of his flat in Adelphi Terrace by a London newspaper reporter about the drowning of two undergraduate students from Oxford. He'd been on his way to post his latest letter to Michael when the reporter, oblivious to Barrie's unknowing, ended up being the one to inform him that those two students were Michael Llewelyn Davies and his friend Rupert Buxton.

The two young men had drowned while bathing in the River Thames at Sandford Pool. Michael was a month short of his twenty-first birthday. Upon understanding the weight of what had happened, Barrie quietly returned to his flat.

Michael had never learned how to swim properly and in fact never shifted his fear of water either. Therefore, his decision to go swimming in the part of the river that was labelled with warnings about previous drownings and being a dangerous spot for swimming, is unknown.

Two men working at a paper-mill had witnessed the pair's drowning. One stated the following:

> *'I heard a shout... I looked in the direction and saw two men bathing in the pool in difficulties... Their heads were close together: they were sort of standing in the water and not struggling.'* [When asked if he formed the impression that they were clasped] *'Yes, that was my impression.'* [13]

The water was 6 – 9 metres deep but reportedly still that day according to the two men.

From the witness statements and the fact that Michael was known not to be able to swim, both deaths were concluded as 'accidental drowning', and that Rupert Buxton had been trying to save Michael when he ended up drowning himself. Both bodies were recovered the following afternoon.

When faced with the rumour that Michael and Rupert's deaths had been a suicide pact, Nico later wrote:

> *'I've always had something of a hunch that Michael's death was suicide. He was in a way the "type" – exceptionally clever, subject to long fits of depression. I'm apt to think – stressing think – that he was going through something of a homosexual phase and maybe let this get a bigger hold on his thinking than it need: I have no knowing of Rupert's leanings in this direction, but I would guess they preferred each other's company to anyone else's.'* [14]

Of course, it's not concrete evidence and nothing can be proven for or against the theory that Michael was gay and struggled heavily with his sexuality. On the other hand, all the indicators throughout his life still lead us to the conclusion that he and Rupert had shared more than just a platonic friendship, and that the drowning of them both was not an accident.

Michael was afraid of water. He wouldn't go near big stretches of it. The idea that he would suddenly be comfortable with bathing in the river is too unbelievable. He was also known – and quoted to – suffer from depression, so if he was battling with accepting his sexuality and furthermore himself, these factors only would've added to it.

Perhaps, during the few days in Dorset with Rupert, the pair had reached a pinnacle in their relationship, along with the understanding that in their society, they would never be accepted. At this point, with both suffering from depression, it's likely that the suicidal intent had crept in, and they could see no other option. They chose to die together, without the world knowing a single thing.

Barrie could not accept the concept of Michael having taken his own life, especially when he'd loved him so deeply and never failed to provide everything he might've needed – Michael had wanted for nothing.

Across the London newspapers in the following days, the headline would read:

THE TRAGEDY OF PETER PAN
SIR J. M. BARRIE'S LOSS OF AN ADOPTED SON[15]

Michael Llewelyn Davies, the face of Peter Pan, was halted in his youth, forever-young, just like the fictional boy that wouldn't grow up.

Chapter 16

To die will be an awfully big adventure
1921–1937

The first people that Barrie contacted after hearing of Michael's drowning was Gerald du Maurier, the boys' grandfather, and Peter. They both travelled to Barrie's flat straight away. He also telephoned his secretary Cynthia Asquith, who was taken aback by Barrie's tone of voice.

Cynthia arrived on the scene shortly after Gerald and Peter to find Barrie inconsolable and in shock. He seemed not to hear when any of them spoke to him and spent the night pacing his study, even continuing this monotonous routine instead of going to bed.

The following morning, Peter took on the grave task of going to Eton to tell Nico what had happened to Michael, bringing him back to Adelphi Terrace the same day. However, as soon as Nico walked in, Barrie cried for him to be taken away, distressed by the sight of him because of how similar he looked to Michael. Nico later talked of this encounter:

> 'Strangely, I don't remember feeling hurt by this, rather did I understand in some way how my very closeness to Michael made his more or less uncontrollable grief even more uncontrollable...'[1]

Nico was eighteen years old at the time of Michael's death, still a child in the eyes of many. During his short life he'd already lost his mother, father, and two of his brothers. If Barrie was inconsolable, Nico somehow kept things together very well.

Nico did go on to tell Mary Hodgson of Michael's death, travelling to the hospital where she was now working as a midwife to break the news.

To die will be an awfully big adventure

He admitted to sobbing in a doorway with her. Jack had also been informed of his younger brother's death by this point.

After the inquest had taken place and the cause of death officially ruled as 'accidental drowning', Michael's body was taken to Barrie's flat to be kept until the funeral. Barrie continued not to sleep for two days, and Cynthia voluntarily took over as much as she was able in caring for him and making arrangements, disconcerted by how the Scotsman:

'...looked like a man in a nightmare.' [2]

She summoned a doctor to prescribe him a sleeping draught that would help him get some rest and kept a sharp vigilance over him, even when he shut himself away in his room and refused to speak to anyone. It was apparent that those days after Michael's death were high-risk for Barrie, that he was thinking of taking his own life as well.

'To die will be an awfully big adventure.'

This is what Barrie wrote in *Peter and Wendy*, when Peter was facing drowning on Marooners' Rock. Now, this quote was more profound than ever for the writer himself. Two of his boys had taken this route too young, and for Barrie this was the only route left for himself now that Michael was gone, even though Jack, Peter and Nico were still living, Nico still being in school. Without Michael, there was no Peter Pan, and no adventures left.

Michael's funeral took place on 23rd May. He was buried close to his parents in Hampstead Churchyard. Roger Senhouse attended along with some of Michael's other peers from Oxford, and he was reported to have been led away from the funeral sobbing.

In the following weeks, Barrie was disconnected from reality and did not come to acknowledge how he had been with the people around him until several months afterwards; he was completely wrapped up in his own grief to take much note of anyone else's. In a letter to Elizabeth Lucas, he wrote in December 1921:

'All the world is different to me now. Michael was pretty much my world.' [3]

In another letter to Michael's tutor at Oxford, he wrote:

> '...what happened was in a way the end of me...'[4]

Haunted by Michael's death, he wrote the following lines in his personal notebooks in the coming years:

> '- Michael. On 7th November 1922 I dreamt that he came back to me, not knowing that he was drowned and that I kept this knowledge from him, and we went on for another year in old way till the fatal 19TH approached again & he became very sad not knowing why, and I feared what was to happen but never let on...'[5]

These notes went on to say how in this dream, Michael would return every year as if nothing had happened, then return to the pool on the anniversary without fail to drown. Further notes on the dream and his thoughts around it highlighted the confused emotions he was feeling around the circumstances of the young man's death:

> '-How in agony I had to let him go away sometimes to live ordinary life of ~~young~~ youth
>   -His gallant fear of water which he confides to me in the extra year. (How this affects me...)
>   -Must be clear tht there is nothing suicidal about it.
>   -Effect on my own life. Give up ordinary work – he chides me for laziness – His joy of living greater than ever – ecstasy of childhood comes back.
>   -It is as if long after writing 'P. Pan' its true meaning came to me – Desperate attempt to grow up but can't.
>   -A love affair? ...How would I treat it seeing I think he will go again?'

The last couple of notes here are suggestive that Barrie finally understood himself and, in that respect, understood Michael. When he mentions 'a love affair', he is not talking about himself with Michael, but Michael and Rupert. It's here that he sees himself in an honest light for the first time as someone that wants to mentally grow up but just can't make himself, and if he accepts that to be the truth then maybe Michael wasn't the societal norm, either.

Furthermore, if Michael and Rupert had been involved romantically, it would change Barrie's view and insistence that their deaths were not by suicide, to the possibility that it was. Plus, with all the supporting factors and questions surrounding the incident, this realisation would've been a second blow to Barrie.

In *Peter and Wendy*, Peter says, 'I want always to be a little boy and to have fun.' a line that Barrie describes as 'his greatest pretend'. As a reflection of himself, the pretense was over; Michael was gone, and so were the days of trying to recapture his youth in every potential corner. Multiple people close to Barrie said that he was never the same after Michael's death, and Nico especially quoted:

> *'Uncle Jim told me that I understood him better than anyone else alive... yet I realised that I could never be a substitute for all that he had lost. When Michael died, the light of his life went out.'*[6]

As for the remaining Llewelyn Davies brothers, they were hit quite hard by another brother's death. Nico particularly struggled because he'd been the closest to Michael in his final years – just as Peter had been with George before George's death – and having to remain living in Barrie's flat during the holidays with his grief-stricken Uncle Jimmy only made things all the more difficult. Michael's ghost was everywhere.

In fact, Barrie was even a little ruthless about Nico in the way he compared him to Michael. Nico followed Michael's footsteps to Oxford University after finishing his schooling at Eton, and in a letter to Robin Dundas – Michael's former tutor – Barrie wrote:

> *'[Nico] is not of course a Michael, life has so far presented no problems to him, nothing terrible and nothing thrillingly joyous such as Michael saw... He will never probably be 'intellectual' in any prominent way, but he is able I think in the sense that he has a powerful brain, and he is very lovable and a true admirer of the fine things... He has not*

read greatly but has good taste in poetry especially and likes to hear it talked of by those who care for it. Most of his reticence is owing to his passionate regard for Michael. He has a sort of childish fear of breaking down when that name is mentioned. Nevertheless the more it is mentioned to him the better I am pleased. He is very emotional and frightened thereat.'[7]

This is an incredibly harsh judgement against Nico, who should not have been treated as the shadow of his brother, as well as the ignorance towards how Nico dealt with Michael's death. For Barrie to call him 'childish' is hypocritical, and to dismiss how upset Nico would get by mentioning Michael's name by mentioning it more just because it pleased him is insensitive to say the least.

If Barrie is guilty of anything, it is this insensitivity. It's normal for people to become selfish in their grief but that doesn't make such behaviour any less unacceptable. Overall, Barrie is afforded no excuses here.

Besides, Barrie and the remaining Llewelyn Davies boys weren't the only ones to experience intensive grief from Michael's death. Robert Boothby – Lord Boothby by the time he made the following statement in 1976 – said:

'When Michael died, I received a number of hysterical letters from friends, the most hysterical being from Edward Marjoribanks... I'm convinced that Edwards's own suicide a few years later was motivated by Michael's death... As for myself, I've made a pretty good mess of my life, which would have been very different if Michael had lived. He had a great influence over me, more than anyone else I've ever known. He would have stopped me doing many foolish things. He would have kept me on the rails.'[8]

Nico also attended Oxford University from 1922 as Michael had, another place that would've been haunted by Michael's previous presence. Whether he decided to go to Oxford as a way to impress Barrie or because he wanted to feel closer to Michael, is unknown. It's even likely he attended Oxford purely for his own merit.

To die will be an awfully big adventure

Nico stayed with Barrie in Adelphi Terrace for another five years, from Michael's death until 1926, when he moved out of the London flat to marry Mary James.

Although Nico never really spoke badly of Barrie in the years that followed, there's no doubt that this was a difficult time period for him – none of the remaining brothers were there for companionship and feeling in constant comparison to Michael only would've taken its toll on the youngest Llewelyn Davies brother and his sense of individuality and self-esteem.

Meanwhile, Jack was still happily married to Gerrie, and they soon had two children: Timothy in 1921, then Sylvia – respectively named after Jack's mother – in 1924. Then, in 1931, Peter was the last to become engaged and marry; to Margaret Ruthven in 1931. At this point, Barrie commented:

'...my task is over and the long day is done.'[9]

Since all three of the remaining boys were now independent and settled, what with being married and starting families of their own, Barrie felt that his responsibility of being their guardian and seeing them raised after their parents had died was accomplished. He kept in touch with all of them quite regularly through letters, though of course the visits weren't always as frequent as Barrie may have liked.

Eventually, Barrie began to live better with his grief. Although he now lived completely alone – still at Adelphi Terrace – he went on to meet a vast number of fellow celebrities throughout his career, including Charlie Chaplin and Mary Pickford.

His dreams of getting more involved with motion pictures also came into being in 1924, when he signed over the film rights for Peter Pan to *Paramount Pictures*. They in turn produced a silent film (*Peter Pan*, 1924[10]) with a soundtrack and subtitles that was based on the original play. Barrie did write a screenplay for the film as he was quite involved in the production, however, the director Herbert Brenon rejected Barrie's pages and hired Willis Goldbeck to write the screenplay instead. Barrie did, at least, get the final say on casting, choosing Betty Bronson to star as Peter along with Ernest Torrence as Captain Hook, Mary Brian as Wendy Darling, and Virginia Brown Faire as Tinker Bell.

This first film of *Peter Pan* was largely Americanised, what with the Darling family actually living in the United States instead of London,

England, and the US flag being flown rather than the standard pirate skull and crossbones. This didn't seem to bother Barrie, however, as he was just excited to finally see his story as a motion picture. The new medium fascinated him so much, and *Peter Pan* was finally a part of it.

In later years, in the looming shadow cast by the oncoming Second World War, Barrie also got involved with speaking out against Hitler and hosted lunches for Winston Churchill and other political figures of the time. The range of his interests and passions from the stage into politics made him a key figure for the general public, who were still recovering from the aftermath of the First World War.

Then, in 1929, Sir James Barrie donated the copyright to *Peter Pan* – of both the book and the play – to Great Ormond Street Children's Hospital, so that they would always receive funds for the incredible work they did (and still do) for sick children. It was a cause that Barrie felt strongly for and one that should be considered as the greatest charitable donation made by such a public figure – they still receive funds from Peter Pan's legacy today.

In an interview with Sarah Ferguson for a featurette covering the production of *Peter Pan* (2003), Nico's daughter, Laura, was asked why Barrie had donated the rights to his most loved story. She replied:

> *'I think he thought it would be a wonderful thing to do. I mean children [had] always meant a lot to him, more he related to children much better than he did to grown-ups. Always.'* [11]

Along with this donation, Barrie requested that the total figure of royalties they received never be released to the public, and despite there being a few rumours circulating on the amount of money raised so far, this condition is still honoured to this day.

Barrie's donation has been marked as Barrie's biggest kindness; being remembered for bringing Peter Pan to the world is what he is renowned for, but second to that is what he did for Great Ormond Street Hospital. *Peter Pan* was his biggest financial success internationally, the work that massively boosted his career and had him known the world over by children and adults alike – and he gave it all away. In a way, it's almost as if he was done with it; it seemed to have brought him more sadness than it had joy and he wanted to be rid of it. But ultimately, this is a gift that millions of

To die will be an awfully big adventure

sick children have benefitted from, and amazingly continue to, which is a legacy that Barrie would be most proud to have left.

Barrie continued to remain popular with children as he grew older. Nico had a daughter in 1928 called Laura, whom Barrie was anointed Godfather of; he was quite present in her life for her early years, as Nico was keen to keep him around. Peter also now had two sons: Ruthven, who was born in 1933 and George, named after Peter's brother, born in 1935.

Barrie's admiration among children even took his acquaintances to the royal family, as he befriended Princess Margaret when she was three years old. The young princess claimed to be Barrie's 'greatest friend' and even contributed a few lines to Barrie's last play – he'd noted them down in conversation, and openly gave her the credit for them. He playfully drew up a contract with Margaret that said she would receive a penny for each night the play was performed on stage.

This gag between them extended so far as King George VI – her father – sending Barrie a message 'warning' him that if the pennies owed to Margaret were not paid, then His Majesty's solicitors would be getting involved. Barrie was pleasantly amused by the notion and planned to take the bag of pennies for Princess Margaret to Buckingham Palace himself – except he never got the chance.

On 21st June 1937, J.M. Barrie passed away from pneumonia.

'He was tired. He wanted to go.'[12]

Nico was with him – as was Peter – at the nursing home in Marylebone where he was being cared for.

Barrie was seventy-seven.

❋

The final play that Barrie wrote was called *The Boy David*.[13] It followed the story of King David of the Bible, who died in childhood.

Through this play, Barrie brought his life in a full circle to its end, back at the beginning; he never forgot his older brother David, the first boy in his life who would never grow up. Now, Barrie was joining him, aged in body but forever young in his mind and spirit.

Chapter 17

I suppose it's like the ticking crocodile, isn't it? Time is chasing after all of us
1937–1980

The death of Sir James Barrie was naturally followed by a national and international mourning, for Peter Pan's creator was dead. From starting his life in a small town in the North of Scotland to being loved by children and respected by adults worldwide, it was a loss to the world of theatre and publishing. The headlines read:

**Sir James Barrie,
Creator of Peter Pan,
Dies at 77**

His body was taken back to his birthplace in Kirriemuir for burial, where he was to be laid to rest with his parents, his sister and other relatives in the town cemetery. His funeral took place on 24th June.

The procession for the event was the length of the town, with a range of people in attendance from the local residents to the obvious immediate connections: Jack, Peter and Nico. Also present were some famous names, Ramsey MacDonald being the key political representative.

To be returned to the place where Barrie had been a child as his final destination was the most fitting end for the man who couldn't grow up.

When it came to his assets, Barrie had already left the copyright for all the Peter Pan works to Great Ormond Street Children's Hospital, so when it came to his vast fortune most of his remaining legacy went to his secretary, Cynthia Asquith. He then of course left Jack, Peter, and Nico a decent sum

I suppose it's like the ticking crocodile, isn't it?

each in his will, as well as his ex-wife, Mary Ansell, an annuity for the remainder of her life.

The year after Barrie's death, Peter's youngest child was born in 1938 and was named Peter; due to adult Peter's well-known feelings of being heavily associated with Barrie's creation, we have to assume that he did not name his son after the famed boy in the stories, but after himself as a way to take back the name. In a later interview, Peter's oldest son Ruthven, said of his father's relationship with the story:

> '*My father had mixed feelings about the whole business of Peter Pan. He accepted that Barrie considered that he was the inspiration for Peter Pan and it was only reasonable that my father should inherit everything from Barrie. That was my father's expectation. It would have recompensed him for the notoriety he had experienced since being linked with Peter Pan – something he hated.*'[1]

Peter was clearly quite bitter about the fact that he hadn't been left more of a financial gift from Barrie in the event of his death, especially since it was his own namesake that was used to represent the famous story. It's an understandable complaint coming from an adopted son, especially when he hated being associated with Peter Pan as much as he did and the years since it was first staged had not brought him any joy.

Peter had, at least, had Barrie's help to set up a publishing house in 1926 – no doubt with the writer's expertise and good contacts – called *Peter Davies Ltd*. It was through this that he was able to publish one of the works of his cousin, Daphne du Maurier: *The Young George du Maurier; A Selection of His Letters 1860-67*.

In 1950, Peter finished compiling a vast number of family papers and letters into a collection which he called the *Morgue*. It was a book that he never wanted published and only reproduced it for select family members and friends. Most of the copies he made, he ended up burning. He originally pitched the idea to his brothers Jack and Nico, writing to them in a letter:

> '*As you know, I have a good many letters and documents relating to dead members of our family and to our "guardian", JMB. And I find, and believe you agree with me, that the best*

thing on the whole to do with all such papers is to destroy them, particularly when their general effect is depressing rather than stimulating or merely entertaining. But on the other hand I have noticed in myself, as I get older, an increasing inclination to take an interest in "the day before yesterday", and the day before that. I believe this is quite a common phenomenon. Such an interest has a way of becoming the stronger, as one's relatives of the older generation, who could have told one so much, become estranged or die... If you think the whole thing a mistake, you can always tear it up and throw it away, as I shall now proceed to tear up and throw away the letters... '[2]

Among the hundreds of letters that he waded through were those shared between Michael and Barrie, which he ended up destroying without documenting.

It's thought that although he claimed to be compiling this collection for the sake of providing some history for his children should they show interest in the past of their family, that going through the letters and documents of his late parents and brothers and guardian was to settle some question he held himself.

It's even more likely that this process was one that only caused more of an impact on his poor mental health.

Although the *Morgue* was never officially published – even to this day is upheld by the wishes of Peter's sons – the general compilation is available on the J.M. Barrie archive, the website[3] entrusted to Andrew Birkin by Great Ormond Street Hospital.

Peter was never able to escape his link to Barrie's story, and it plagued him all throughout his life. The toll this took on him was accompanied by underlying health issues, as he suffered from Emphysema, a lower respiratory disease caused by enlarged air-filled spaces in the lungs. He was also an alcoholic. All these factors caused him to suffer from a great depression that was already known to have troubled two of his brothers, one of which was a suspected suicide despite the 'accidental' ruling.

Then, on 17th September 1959, Jack passed away from lung disease. He was sixty-five.

Jack had been living in Northern Cornwall with his wife and had lived a life relatively peacefully and separate from the Peter Pan legacy. It was

I suppose it's like the ticking crocodile, isn't it?

this loss to Peter that was quite possibly what tipped him over the edge, in the end.

Just seven months afterward on 5th April 1960, Peter threw himself under a London Underground train that was pulling into Sloane Square Station and died.

For Peter, Barrie's involvement with his family had ultimately only caused him misery. Only his very young childhood years seemed to be his happiest, before *Peter Pan* took off at the theatre, the magic of the games with Barrie wore off and the playwright took his name for a character that would be known the world over:

> *'...in the end, his connection with our family brought so much more sorrow than happiness.'*[4]

Despite it being known that Peter wasn't keen on being referred to as Peter Pan, or even the inspiration for the famous character, newspapers still broadcast the news of his death with the following range of headlines:

'Inspiration of 'Peter Pan' Dies in Accident in London Subway'
'Peter Pan's Death Leap'
'The Boy Who Never Grew Up Is Dead'

Even in death, he couldn't escape it.

Now the only surviving brother of the Llewelyn Davies boys, Nico became the sole representative of Barrie and the origins of the Peter Pan legacy. He was happy to be involved when it came to talking about the subject and was even a consultant writer for the BBC series *The Lost Boys*,[5] a biographical drama that aired in 1978. This series was written by Andrew Birkin, mentioned previously, who is a renowned expert on J.M. Barrie.

The Lost Boys (1978) was an extremely accurate portrayal of J.M. Barrie and his life, following the events of his meeting the Llewelyn Davies family and onwards. In three parts totalling over four and a half hours, the TV mini-series went into great details of Barrie's strange marriage to Mary Ansell as well as how his life was shaped from the five Llewelyn Davies boys. With Nico there to guide the writing, it's an excellent depiction that incorporates Barrie's own notes and letters, accompanied by excellent acting all round but particularly Ian Holm, who played Barrie himself. It was received with high praise and went on to be nominated for various awards, as well as winning a BAFTA in 1979 and three Royal Television Society awards.

After the series was aired and it proved a great success, Birkin went on to write a thorough biography of Barrie: *J.M. Barrie and the Lost Boys* (1979), in which Nico actually gave him access to the Llewelyn Davies family archive. Much of this is now available to the public, so it is thanks to Nico and his allowance to share these documents and letters with Birkin that we have been able to truly look into the life and mind of J.M. Barrie.

Nico lived until the age of seventy-six, passing away on 14th October 1980.

His legacy is continued by his daughter and only child, Laura, now known as Laura Duguid. She is still living as of 2023 at the age of ninety-five.

Laura has spoken about her father Nico, along with Barrie whom she also referred to as Uncle Jim, in numerous interviews. She was nine years old when Barrie died so has some memories of him. Most notably, she was interviewed by Sarah Ferguson, the Duchess of York, in 2003, where she eagerly advocated for the story of *Peter Pan* in all its forms:

> *'The start of it was really a book called 'The Little White Bird', where the story of Peter Pan begins evolving and there's also 'Peter Pan and Wendy', the book. The play is very much still there but Peter Pan is the thing that people know and the thing that will really last.'*[6]

She also went on to say how excited 'Uncle Jim' would be by all the modern special effects they were able to do for the movie *Peter Pan* (2003), since he had shown an interest in motion pictures when they were first becoming popular.

Laura even made a cameo in the movie *Finding Neverland* (2004), a biopic about J.M. Barrie and the nature of his relationship with Sylvia Llewelyn Davies and her sons, starring Johnny Depp as Barrie and Kate Winslet as Sylvia. The movie wasn't very historically accurate as it depicted Barrie divorcing Mary Ansell over romantic feelings towards Sylvia which simply wasn't true, and Nico's existence was completely erased. Barrie's favourite of the boys was also depicted to be Peter instead of Michael for the sake of the plot.

I suppose it's like the ticking crocodile, isn't it?

Laura is the only surviving member of the Llewelyn Davies family line that knew Barrie personally.

Through the decades there have been numerous documentaries, articles and biographies that have explored Barrie's life and work, many of which have analysed the kind of person he was. Some publications looked at him in a favourable light because of the charitable work he did for children as well for bringing *Peter Pan* to the world, whilst others have not been so kind.

To deconstruct a lot of the negative speculation that surrounds his name, the aim of this book has hopefully proved that Barrie was in no way inappropriate with children, only belonged amongst them, an 'innocent' as Nico described him. He loved the Llewelyn Davies boys deeply and his relationship with them was between paternal and platonic: he saw them as friends when he first met them and as they grew and lost both their parents, they became more like sons.

Due to the time's perception of affection between men, Barrie was never ever able to openly express his love for the boys with the likes of embraces or words of affection. His outlet of this suppressed love came through his writing instead, which in modern assessment has been often perceived as perverted.

Barrie has received slander from other writers claiming that he was a 'monster that didn't love'[8] when on the contrary, he did love and deeply, just not romantically – for which he has been unjustly criminalised. Of course, he played around flirtatiously with actresses as if he were a young boy, enjoying the attention he received as a result and the game of the chase, even going so far as to marry someone in order to please society. But in the end, he knew that he did not love his wife in the way she wanted – the way she deserved – and when she was unfaithful and wanted to leave, he inevitably let her.

He did admire women, particularly for their capability as mothers, so that even when it came to Sylvia he mostly just loved her in the same way a brother might love a sister. His claims of their engagement after her death were more likely to have come from a place of concern for the five boys left without her rather than a romantic attraction; the worry that the boys would be taken away from him took precedence here.

Then there's Barrie's childishness: it was genuine throughout his life, as was his ability to make friends with children. Unlike the similar author Lewis Carroll, who only made friends with young girls and not boys as his 'child friends', Barrie loved all children and his interactions with them were only ever innocent. Carroll, meanwhile, was reported to have taken inappropriate photographs of the Liddell sisters.

Additionally, Barrie related to children better than he ever did adults because he was never able to mature in the way the others around him had; he continued to enjoy the same things children did even though he'd left his childhood behind and as a result, was on a level of understanding with them. This meant he was more popular company with children than he ever was with adults. All these factors are key evidence in Barrie being the first person recorded to have lived with Peter Pan Syndrome, a psychological state that his own story ended up providing the name for. He would never know of this.

Perhaps if Barrie had been born in a later time period, he would've had a better understanding of himself earlier on, with the opportunity to be understood and accepted by society in return. Despite all the fame and success he derived in his life, he lost so much when it came to the people he loved and never really recovered from his grief. The bereavements started when he was so young and they plagued him until his final years.

Many believe that Barrie's involvement with the Llewelyn Davies boys is what led to their misery and even some of their deaths, but that crowd do not consider that Barrie only created the world and the characters and the story. The public and the press are the ones that ran with the idea that the boys were at the heart of it – which of course they were – but it was inconsiderate to thrust such an image onto children in that way. Peter's suicide in 1960, for example, was due to a number of factors including the association with Peter Pan; the consistent relation made by the public and the paparazzi wasn't ignited by Barrie. Michael's possible struggle with his sexuality is traced back to an unaccepting society, not Barrie. George was killed in a war caused by men in power, not Barrie, and Jack's feelings of segregation from his family were because he was sent away from a young age, a decision not made by his Uncle Jimmy.

Nico was the only one that was hurt by Barrie in the end with being cruelly compared to Michael so much.

> I suppose it's like the ticking crocodile, isn't it?

Plus, there are more examples of children like the Llewelyn Davies boys that grew up with such an association. To begin with, Rupert Buxton (Michael's companion whom he'd drowned with) had previously been close acquaintances with Alastair Grahame, the son of Kenneth Grahame – author of *The Wind in the Willows*.[9] Kenneth Grahame had always claimed his son to be the basis of the character Mr Toad, and this association followed Alistair around right from publication. Even his peers at Oxford University referred to him by the nickname 'Toad'. With blindness in one eye and a string of health issues, Alistair did not handle the fame and attention so well, and committed suicide on 7th May 1920 by laying down on a railway track until a train ran him over. He was nineteen. At the time, his death was ruled 'accidental'.

Similarly, A.A. Milne – author of the *Winnie-the-Pooh*[10] stories – used his son Christopher Robin for a complete mold of his character that was also named Christopher Robin. Although Christopher Robin mostly loved the charming stories and lived a full life, he was reported to hate the fame and association that *Winnie-the-Pooh* had brought to him after he was bullied relentlessly throughout his school years.

To conclude, using children as inspiration for stories and then outing them as such is something that should never be trusted to the general public.

Barrie should continue to be remembered for bringing a story that is so complex in themes and characterisation that it has continued to fascinate readers over 100 years after it was first presented to audiences. The world he created will be enjoyed by adults and children alike for many years more.

Additionally, as much joy as it has brought to the young generations of the world, it predominantly brings grown-ups back to their own childhoods, providing the nostalgia of not wishing to grow up so often missed in old age. They can remember the endless boundaries of the imagination, feel in awe of magical beings like fairies and mermaids and for just a short time feel the hope and joy that most children do before they are exposed to the horrors of the real world.

As Barrie wrote for the closing lines of *Peter and Wendy*, the story of Peter Pan will always be a timeless one thanks to him, a man who lost so much but always maintained the eye to see the good in the world, as long as children continue to be 'gay and innocent and heartless'.

Epilogue

The Peter Pan legacy has lived on through various means almost one hundred years after Barrie's death, and the story is just as alive as it was if not even more.

The book, *Peter and Wendy*, is now mainly reprinted with the reduced title of *Peter Pan*, just as Frohman had wanted the stage play to be. It's a book that has never been out of print; numerous reprints from various publishing houses, all with different illustrations and cover designs are in circulation from simple paperback editions to elaborate hardbacks with valuable bindings. Along with picture-books, comic books and graphic novels, there have also been annotated versions of the story for the more literary scholar, alongside a string of analytical essays.

A number of authors have also pitched in their own ideas to write sequels, prequels and reimagining's that have all proven popular with young and adolescent audiences. Most notably is *Peter Pan in Scarlet*,[1] classed as 'the official sequel' written by Geraldine McCaughrean. Its writing and publication was authorised by Great Ormond Street and understandably so, since the character personalities and setting of Neverland remain extremely loyal to the original text whilst also allowing room for readers to experience more. The loyalty to Barrie's text is unmatched and there have been rumours that the book is set to be adapted to film but, as of 2023, nothing more has surfaced.

Peter Pan or The Boy Who Wouldn't Grow Up continued to run as a Christmas performance on stage long after Barrie left the scene. His personal changes and alterations of the script obviously stopped, but others began to take over instead. The 1937 production – the first without Barrie – was led with Elsa Lanchester as Peter and Charles Laughton as Captain Hook, and for some reason the usual decision to have Mr Darling and Captain Hook played by the same actor was scrapped. Peter Murray-Hill was cast as Mr Darling instead.

Epilogue

The cast did at least start a heartwarming tradition after Barrie donated the rights of *Peter Pan* to Great Ormond Street: every year, they would perform the play inside the hospital for patients and staff in order to honour Barrie's great gift. The story and the funding this has brought to the hospital is predominantly the key factor, as it has been helping children to get well from their illnesses and grow up. This, and the sense of wonderment Peter Pan brings to all audiences, is a legacy that no author could deny being proud of.

As the years went on, the stage performances of *Peter Pan* began to lean away from what the initial script had been, developing into more of a pantomime.

Pantomime: a popular kind of musical comedy performed across theatres around the Christmas period which is aimed towards families, with jokes and quips for both adults and children scattered throughout. Originally sourced from ancient Rome, it developed in Britain to showcase other popular stories such as *Cinderella*, *Snow White and the Seven Dwarves* and *Aladdin*.

Peter Pan already checked a lot of the boxes to fit into the category with the lead hero boy traditionally being played by a woman and Mr Smee providing the comic relief. From here, the original emotionally deeper moments in the story started to get gradually erased along with the intricately fleshed-out characters.

This wasn't really the main cause for Peter Pan's novelty being lost over time, however.

Walter Elias Disney, otherwise known as the famous animator and entrepreneur Walt Disney, had shown interest in the story of Peter Pan since 1935, when Barrie was still alive. He'd seen one of the original performances of *Peter Pan* at a theatre in the US when he was ten years old, when Maude Adams headlined as Peter, and even played the title character himself in a school production. All this generated his early enjoyment of the story so that when he began releasing animated shorts, he was extremely keen to adapt Peter Pan. In fact, Walt Disney wanted to make an animated feature of Peter Pan before *Snow White and the Seven Dwarfs*[2] (Disney's first full-length animated movie) was even put into production and later released in

1937. Unfortunately, he never got to meet or discuss his ideas with Barrie, which could have changed the movie from what we know today.

Walt's brother, Roy Disney, visited Great Ormond Street Children's Hospital in April 1937 to inquire about obtaining the rights to the play to be adapted to film, but by then they had just sold them to *Paramount Pictures*. Over the following year and a half, Disney worked on obtaining the rights himself, eventually buying them from *Paramount* in October 1938. By 1939, he'd signed a contract with the hospital, too.

Organising the story was now able to commence, and the initial plan was to tell Peter's backstory starting in Kensington Gardens. Eventually this was scrapped to stay loyal to Barrie's order of events.

One action that Disney took to stay as respectful to the author's wishes as possible was to reach out to Maude Adams in 1940 to ask if she might view an early reel of the film. It was in the very early production stages at the time, and Adams ended up rejecting the offer on the grounds that Peter was to her 'real life and blood, while another's creation of this character would only be a ghost'.[3] Disney was extremely disappointed by her response, claiming that she was being 'silly' and 'living in the past'. Realistically, Adams was being protective over the story on behalf of Barrie, which is understandable considering she worked with the author so closely. Regardless, Disney went ahead with the project without her blessing.

It took another thirteen years before an animated adaptation was released, what with delays from the Second World War and several other of Disney's projects taking precedence. *Walt Disney's Peter Pan*[4] premiered in theatres on 5th February 1953.

To date, Disney's animated version has had a lifetime gross of approximately $427.5 million, and it set the new standard for what the story and the characters were capable of. It rewrote the feel of the story to be a watered-down version of Barrie's creation, with the darker themes being mostly glossed over and replaced with a whimsical cartoon, the main intention being to easily entertain. Peter's key character traits – his selfishness and lack of empathy – aren't very apparent in the film, and Captain Hook is portrayed more as a comedic coward rather than the ruthless and genuinely terrifying villain he was written to be. The musical numbers also tone down the gloomier themes to be more light-hearted, despite one of these songs having racist tendencies towards Native Americans by referring to them as 'redskins', a stereotype not acceptable by today's standards – or indeed ever, despite its usage in the past.

Bosley Crowther of *The New York Times* did actually criticize the film's lack of faithfulness to the original play, claiming:

> '...it has the story but not the spirit of Peter Pan as it was plainly conceived by its author...'[5]

The Walt Disney Company went on to release a sequel to the animated feature in 2002, thirty-six years after their founder died, called *Peter Pan in: Return to Neverland*,[6] which didn't depict the Natives of Neverland at all due to the previous backlash. It was even more light-hearted and 'fun' than the first and wasn't very popular with critics. It did, however, explore the character of Jane, Wendy's daughter, beyond Barrie's addition of 'When Wendy Grew Up'. The story follows her very opposite desire not to stay young and her struggle to be a child and retain her innocence in the midst of the Second World War. It's an interesting take, which it should at least be given credit for, especially considering Barries involvement with the wounded children on the battlefront of France in the First World War.

Disney's commercialisation of Peter Pan continued when they decided to trademark the character of Tinker Bell. Her popularity first led her to becoming an iconic mascot for the Walt Disney Company, stamped on the Disney Park logos and merchandise almost as much as Mickey Mouse, becoming a key representative for the company. This continued when she was placed into her own film series that started in 2005 and was aimed at an even younger audience; the Disney Fairies franchise presented Tinker Bell to be kind, selfless, thoughtful, and adventurous. This version of the character isn't in any way a resemblance of Barrie's creation, but a new model with the same name designed to make modern audiences happier.

Barrie's Tinker Bell is widely known to be spiteful, jealous and streaked with a little murderous spirit. People are often surprised to learn that she was written to have taken part in fairy orgies in the book.

Since Disney were the first filmmakers to majorly popularise Peter Pan commercially on-screen, it is their version and their franchise that have set the tone for most of the future adaptations that continue to miss the mark of J.M. Barrie's original tale. There have been many revisions since Disney's animated movie to the present day – too many to note and analyse each of them – from children's TV shows that focus on the adventures of Peter and the Darling children in Neverland to anime remakes.

Some modern retellings or alternate genre takes did not promise to be loyal to the source material, therefore amount no criticism for straying from the classic. Adaptations that qualify in these categories include *Neverland*[7] (2003) and the upcoming *Peter Pan's Neverland Nightmare*[8] (2024). There is also *Wendy*[9] (2020), which is a dark fantasy take that twists much of the source material to create a very different plot, using lore and myth to showcase Neverland rather than children's imaginations. The presence of pirates and fairies is non-existent and the island is entirely run by children, save for a few adults that lost their faith and their ability to not age. This is an adaptation that sits well as a stand-alone story, that merely took inspiration from Barrie's work, particularly as it made no promises to stay faithful to the original.

Other movie versions, however, have claimed to be working from Barrie's original texts with the intention of remaining loyal to the themes and story, only to completely stray from what Barrie's Peter represented.

A popular interpretation of the Peter Pan story is *Hook* (1991), the famous and popular Steven Spielberg adaptation. The story follows the idea that Peter would choose to grow up after falling in love with Wendy's granddaughter, Moira. Despite inclinations from Barrie's notes to experiment with the idea of Peter Pan growing up, it's quite a stray from a character who does not understand romantic love. Robin Williams as Peter is still widely loved, however, and his nonetheless incredible performance cannot be faulted for any inaccurate writing.

The colourful sets that were used in the film paints Neverland more like a theme park than a magical island – which the film did receive some criticism for – though it does capture much of the era's charm of the nineties, making it unique to its own. This choice of set was also an interesting decision for the sake of appealing to more of an American audience, a feat that has often changed the story of *Peter Pan* to pander to US fans.

Dustin Hoffman's Captain Hook is at least a very close rendition to Barrie's idea of the pirate, being more fearful than Disney's version and using direct quotes from the play and book. With the fear of the ticking crocodile leading to every clock and watch in Neverland being destroyed, as well as the deeper exploration of Hook's feelings towards being hated,

Epilogue

there's something more brought to the story than just a pirate that's the nemesis of Peter Pan.

Additionally, the film does play tribute to people from Barrie's life with the naming of some of the characters. Jack and Maggie, Peter's children in the film, were named after Jack Llewelyn Davies and Barrie's mother, Margaret Ogilvy.

Finally, *Hook* was the first adaptation to introduce a twist on the line 'To die will be an awfully big adventure' with the ending line from Peter being:

'To live will be an awfully big adventure.'[10]

This quote is to place emphasis on the fact that although Peter has left behind a life of adventuring in Neverland, he has chosen to live a normal life in the real world, which in itself is an adventure of its own. Overall, although not completely loyal to Barrie's Peter, *Hook* has redeeming qualities that lie in how fleshed-out the characters are, and audiences remain fond of it.

Another adaptation to utilise the altered version of the quote – 'To live would be an awfully big adventure'[11] – is *Peter Pan* (2003), a live-action telling combining aspects from the book and the play. After Peter has returned Wendy and her brothers' home, Peter watches them from the window and utters these words sadly, and they are conveyed so that the audience can see how much it troubles Peter not to understand what the Darling children have as he gazes at their interaction. It suggests that to live *would* be an adventure for Peter, meaning to leave Neverland and live a normal life. Instead, he chooses to live a life forever in youth, never to experience the kind of love that grown-ups do because it would come with pain and sorrow, and he would rather remain in blasé innocence, experiencing the joys of childhood over and over.

The delivery of this line is just a few seconds of this fantastic adaptation that was directed by P.J. Hogan. It is, in this author's opinion, the best Peter Pan movie that has been made of Barrie's story to date.

To begin with, the director, producers and writers consulted Andrew Birkin, who is already known as a great expert on Barrie and his life, for accuracy on the story. They also spoke with Laura Duguid – Nico's daughter – because she personally remembered the author and what he was like. Together, Laura and Andrew Birkin were able to guide the writing and production process to a result that Barrie would be most proud of.

From here, Native American actors were accurately cast for the roles of Tiger Lily and the natives of Neverland, which hadn't been done before, and incorporated the tradition of having the same actor play both Captain Hook and Mr Darling, a detail that was quite important to Barrie. Jason Isaac's portrayal of Hook finally put forth a character who was actually presented as dangerous to the audience, killing one of his own crew in every other scene and clearly being feared by those around him, without the sense of fear being forcibly acted. He is put before the audience as a true pirate with no worry for the consequences of killing, streaked with a past that needs to only be hinted at to understand.

Most notably is the accurate portrayal of Peter's inability to love romantically. This is the aspect most faithful to Barrie's Peter as it shows the character's tumultuous emotions of not being able to grasp the kind of love Wendy has for him. Jeremy Sumpter's portrayal of Peter Pan is splendidly done as he conveys his lines to show that he feels strongly for Wendy but doesn't understand what it is, and battles with wishing to stay young whilst facing grown-up feelings. In turn, Rachel Hurd-Wood plays Wendy's confusion on how Peter cannot love just as well, which is only antagonised by Hook; the interaction between Hook and Wendy is explored very interestingly here, giving the two more contact in which Wendy's inner conflict is explored by Hook's manipulation. This of course all links back to how she left things with her father at the beginning of the movie.

Peter Pan (2003) also fondly includes a scene to replicate the clapping sequence in the stage play, instead inciting children to chant: 'I do believe in fairies, I do, I do.' It's a warm nod to Barrie's original intention for the story and the history behind the scene.

There are a great number of other perfectly done aspects in this rendition of *Peter Pan* that can studied further, such as the visual effects, and the scenery and lighting being vibrantly coloured and catered to the shifting mood of the story, much like an illustrated storybook. There are the costumes, with Peter covered in skeleton leaves as described in the book, just as the Lost Boys are draped in animal skins and furs, and Captain Hook is vibrantly dressed to represent his station from a life prior to Neverland; the hook on his right hand looks genuinely menacing. The fighting stunts and flying sequences were all done with wires and equipment to use as little CGI possible, and the actors were trained for weeks prior to filming in fencing and 'flying'. All these different parts reflect the charm and magic

Epilogue

and wonder that J.M. Barrie so wished to put across in his story – if there are any criticisms towards this film, they are drowned out by the genuine research and attention and care that went into it.

P.J. Hogan said of the movie:

> *'This is* Peter Pan *as J.M. Barrie originally intended – a heroic, magical, real boy who fights pirates, saves children and never grows up.'* [12]

After such a successfully made adaptation, it has been difficult to top ever since.

In later years, other directors tried their hand at telling the story but with a new angle that began to appear: how did Peter Pan come to Neverland in the first place? How did he and Captain Hook come to be enemies?

Sky Movies released their concept, *Neverland*, in 2011, exploring the idea that Peter Pan and James Hook actually started out as friends. Then, after their discovery of Neverland and being separated from one another, they become involved with different sides of the island – Peter with the natives and Hook with the pirates. They see two different sides and the audience witnesses how they come to hate one another. *Sky Movies'* version also successfully included more of the natives, using Tiger Lily in a more active role than she ever was even in the original story. The lower budget and low-quality special effects and computer-generated scenery can be overlooked due to the success of the unique story telling.

By far the worst adaptation to date is *Pan* (2015). It was utterly disappointing to fans right from early production when the casting was announced and Roony Mara – a Caucasian woman – was cast as Tiger Lily – a Native American. Beyond this main and major mistake (the modern term for this is 'whitewashing'), director Joe Wright gave the impression that the story going to be told would include how Hook and Pan started as friends and became enemies. However, by the end of the film they are still friends and there is no reveal as to how they did turn on one another.

Two Nirvana tracks were shoehorned into the movie which wasn't popularly received, and a number of plot holes left questions that were opened at the beginning of the film unanswered. Although there were mesmerising uses of CGI and special effects, it didn't make up for the poor writing and inaccuracy.

The Dark Side of Peter Pan

The most recent movie adaptation of the Peter Pan story was of course Disney's *Peter Pan and Wendy*[13] (2023). A live-action remake of the 1953 Disney animated original, it was warmly named to include Wendy's name in the title, a reference to Barrie's first naming of the novel, *Peter and Wendy*. Unfortunately, this is generally where the praise for this film ends. Despite the breadth of representation throughout its cast, the story falls flat with a Neverland that resembles nothing like a child's imagination – something that the author confirmed the island is made up of. Instead, this island is no more than a lifeless rock with a dull colour palette. The characters come across as bland with little personality, making them difficult to root for, and beyond the power of flight there is little magical element to Neverland and the people in it. Any incorporation of the book or play felt forced rather than natural.

Wendy's rebellious spirit stands out the most as feeling like a forced trope to appeal to a modern audience, especially when she is such a well-established character already. Many of her lines feel like a cliché and although she's a better role model for newer generations, this is not the motherly character that the author wrote her to be. Tiger Lily is also more prominent in the story and isn't the token damsel in distress. Meanwhile, Peter's character starts relatively well with his cockiness and presumptuous nature being well depicted, but with the plot later offering a history between Peter and Hook being friends, the loyalty to character fades out. As a result of the plot, Peter comes to learn from his mistakes which is against Barrie's creation – he won't grow up, but his learning correlates to growing.

Furthermore, the plot decision to redeem Captain Hook is an unpopular one that has been a common theme across Disney's live-action remakes. The theory that Captain Hook started out as a Lost Boy actually came about from fans of the story, which is an interesting one, yet bringing it into this film cheapens the idea and the story loses the charm of a good-defeating-evil tale. Beyond that, Captain Hook doesn't come across as particularly terrifying as he was written to be, as there is little consequence to crossing him.

There was, at least, a new revision to the famous quote 'To die will be an awfully big adventure':

> *'To grow up... why, it might just be the biggest adventure of all.'*[14]

This does play into the fact that as an audience, we are supposed to want to be Wendy and grow up, to experience life. We are not supposed to want to be Peter Pan.

Overall, the plot of *Peter Pan and Wendy* wasn't very consistent, with Peter complaining of loneliness but ending the film with him returning to Neverland without his Lost Boys, and it defeats the point of Peter's quarrel with Hook. Disney had a great opportunity to add to the cinematic library of this story, but the vision of those who created it once again missed the mark of Barrie's fantastical work.

Each big screen adaptation seems to move further and further from Barrie's *Peter Pan*, so that eventually the original story – the original Peter – will be lost on future generations. Barrie's creation will be filtered through so many interpretations that his Neverland may always be a thing of the past, and it will be difficult for audiences to comprehend what the author intended unless they delve into the history of J.M. Barrie and the Llewelyn Davies family.

On the other hand, having these adaptations – along with books and even video games – is still important in giving all audiences the experience of Peter Pan and Neverland. If Barrie could've seen just how far his story – that had such humble beginnings – would come, particularly when he was so fascinated by motion pictures, he'd be pleased to see the positive effect it's had on the world, specifically for the world's children.

The Peter Pan statue still stands in Kensington Gardens and remains a major tourist attraction, as do the other statues that cropped up in the decades after its initial placement; one stands in Kirriemuir where Barrie was born, and another was appropriately placed outside of Great Ormond Street Children's Hospital.

Of course, Disney had their way with the character too; the ride of *Peter Pan's Flight* is one of the most popular rides at the Disney Parks with the longest wait times, and they have actors playing multiple characters from the story wandering the parks for guests to meet. In this sense, Peter Pan has been immortalised through Disney's commercialisation of it.

Moreover, keeping Barrie's *Peter Pan* alive in turn keeps the author alive. A man whose life consisted of a string of tragedy after tragedy led to the inspiration of a story that has reached every corner of the world, and his audience are the ones that mostly get to reap the profits of what he sowed in terms of the joy it brings. Despite the saddening past and dark history, *Peter Pan* continues to inspire children and adults alike, not only with its wild, imaginative incentive but also with the incredible work it does for Great Ormond Street.

For the funding of the children's hospital alone, James Matthew Barrie would only encourage more adaptations of his story, more ideas, and more interpretations of the famous character to keep the legacy going for many more generations to enjoy.

Sources

Collections

Llewelyn Davies Family Papers. General Collection, Beinecke Rare Book and Manuscript Library, Yale University; consisting of letters, manuscripts and notebooks belonging to Barrie

Peter Llewelyn Davies' *Morgue, Some Davies Letters and Papers, 1874-1915,* made available by Andrew Birkin on the official J.M. Barrie archive website

The Barrie Birthplace Collection, courtesy of The National Trust Scotland

Dolly Ponsonby's unpublished Diaries, 1890-1914, made available by the Dowager Lady Ponsonby to Andrew Birkin, then made available to the public by the latter on the official J.M. Barrie archive website

Personal collection of Geraldine Llewelyn Davies; consisting of letters between herself and Jack, and Jack's letters to Barrie

Books

Ansell, Mary, *Dogs and Men*, (Duckworth & Co., London, 1924)

Barratt, Dan; Trigger, Christine, *The Vanbrugh Sisters: The lives and times of Edwardian actresses Irene and Violet Vanbrugh*, (CreateSpace Independent Publishing Platform, California, 2015)

Barrie, J.M., *Margaret Ogilvy*, (Lightening Source UK Ltd., Milton Keynes, 2022)

Barrie, J.M., *The Wedding Guest*, Collected Works of James M. Barrie, (Classic Books, Middlesex, 2001)

Barrie, J.M., *The Little White Bird*, (Charles Scribners, New York, 1902),

Barrie, J.M., *Peter and Wendy*, (Hodder & Stoughton, London, 1911)

Barrie, J.M., *A Window in Thrums*, (The Saltire Society, Edinburgh, 2005)

Barrie, J.M., *Peter Pan in Kensington Gardens*, (Hodder and Stoughton, London, 1906)

Barrie, J.M., *Peter Pan, or The Boy Who Wouldn't Grow Up, Peter Pan and Other Plays* (Oxford University Press Inc., New York, 2008)

Barrie, J.M., *The Boy David*, (Charles Scribner's Sons, New York, 1938)

Barrie, J.M., *Sentimental Tommy* (Cassell & Company, London, 1896)

Barrie, J.M., *The Little Minister*, (American Publishers Corporation, New York, 1897)

Barrie, J.M., *Tommy and Grizel*, (Createspace, North Charleston, 2004)

Barrie, J.M., *Dear Brutus*, (Hodder and Stoughton, London, 1935)

Barrie, J.M., *The Boy Castaways of Black Lake Island*, (T. and A. Constable, Edinburgh, 1901)

Barry, Dave; Pearson, Ridley, *Peter and the Starcatchers*, (Walker Books Ltd., London, 2006)

Birkin, Andrew, *J.M. Barrie and The Lost Boys*, (Yale University Press, Connecticut, 2003)

Blow, Sydney, *Through the Stage Doors*, (Chambers, London, 1958)

Chase, Pauline, *Peter Pan's Postbag*, (William Heinemann, London, 1909)

Dudgeon, Piers, *The Real Peter Pan: J.M. Barrie and the Boy Who Inspired Him*, (St. Martin's Press, New York, 2015)

Mackail, Denis, *The Story of J.M.B.*, (Peter Davies Ltd., London, 1941)

Marcosson, Isaac F.; Frohman, David, *Charles Frohman: Manager and Man*, (The Bodley Head, London, 1916)

Maude, Pamela, *Worlds Away*, (John Baker, London, 1964)

McCaughrean, Geraldine, *Peter Pan in Scarlet*, (Oxford University Press, Oxford, 2006)

Mixed Authors, *Anthology of Scottish Folktales*, (The History Press, Gloucestershire, 2021)

Tatar, Maria, *The Annotated Peter Pan: The Centennial Edition*, (Norton and Co., New York, 2011)

Websites

The Largest Archive and Database of Scottish Writer J M Barrie, https://jmbarrie.co.uk/

Daily Mail Newspaper Archives, https://www.newspapers.com/

The British Newspaper Archives, https://www.britishnewspaperarchive.co.uk/

Media

Movies
- *Peter Pan* (1924)
- *Peter Pan* (1953)
- *Hook* (1991)
- *Peter Pan in: Return to Neverland* (2002)
- *Peter Pan* (2003)
- *Finding Neverland* (2004)
- *Neverland* (2011)
- *Pan* (2015)
- *Peter Pan and Wendy* (2023)

Television Shows
- *The Lost Boys* (TV Miniseries; 1978)
- *Peter and Wendy* (TV Movie, 2015

Notes

Prologue

1. See *Sources*: Collections, 1
2. Barrie, J.M., *Peter and Wendy*, (Hodder & Stoughton, London, 1911) / Barrie, J.M., *Peter Pan*, (Suzeteo Enterprises, Greenwood, 2019)
3. Spielberg, Steven, *Hook*, (TriStar Pictures, 1991)
4. Willing, Nick, *Neverland*, (Sky Movies, 2011)
5. Wright, Joe, *Pan*, (Warner Bros., 2015)
6. Hogan, P.J., Peter Pan, (Universal Pictures, 2003)

Chapter 1

1. Gibb, Lindsey, Hope, C.A., *The Urisk of Monless Burn, Anthology of Scottish Folktales*, (The History Press, Gloucestershire, 2021), pp. 79-81
2. Taylor, Lea, *The Fairy Boy of Leiff, Anthology of Scottish Folktales*, (The History Press, Gloucestershire, 2021), pp. 116-121
3. Barrie, J.M., *A Window in Thrums*, (The Saltire Society, Edinburgh, 2005)
4. Barrie, J.M., *A Window in Thrums*, (The Saltire Society, Edinburgh, 2005), p. 3
5. Barrie, J.M., *Margaret Ogilvy*, (Lightening Source UK Ltd., Milton Keynes, 2022)
6. Barrie, J.M., *Margaret Ogilvy*, (Lightening Source UK Ltd., Milton Keynes, 2022), pp. 14-15
7. Barrie, J.M., *Margaret Ogilvy*, (Lightening Source UK Ltd., Milton Keynes, 2022), p. 15
8. Barrie, J.M., *Margaret Ogilvy*, (Lightening Source UK Ltd., Milton Keynes, 2022), p. 10

Notes

9. Barrie, J.M., *A Window in Thrums*, (The Saltire Society, Edinburgh, 2005), p. 21
10. Barrie, J.M., *Margaret Ogilvy*, (Lightening Source UK Ltd., Milton Keynes, 2022), p. 5
11. Barrie, J.M., *Margaret Ogilvy*, (Lightening Source UK Ltd., Milton Keynes, 2022), p.6
12. Barrie, J.M., *A Window in Thrums*, (The Saltire Society, Edinburgh, 2005), p. 62
13. Barrie, J.M., *Margaret Ogilvy*, (Lightening Source UK Ltd., Milton Keynes, 2022), p. 7
14. Barrie, J.M., *Margaret Ogilvy*, (Lightening Source UK Ltd., Milton Keynes, 2022), p. 51
15. Barrie, J.M., *Margaret Ogilvy*, (Lightening Source UK Ltd., Milton Keynes, 2022), p. 51
16. Barrie, J.M., *Margaret Ogilvy*, (Lightening Source UK Ltd., Milton Keynes, 2022), p. 7
17. Barrie, J.M., *Margaret Ogilvy*, (Lightening Source UK Ltd., Milton Keynes, 2022), p. 17
18. Barrie, J.M., *Margaret Ogilvy*, (Lightening Source UK Ltd., Milton Keynes, 2022), p. 13
19. See *Sources*: Collections, 1
20. Letter to Mrs Fred Oliver, 21st December 1931
21. See *Sources*: Collections, 1
22. Barrie, J.M., *Margaret Ogilvy*, (Lightening Source UK Ltd., Milton Keynes, 2022), p. 10

Chapter 2

1. Birkin, Andrew, *J.M. Barrie and The Lost Boys*, (Yale University Press, Connecticut, 2003), pp. 11-12
2. Birkin, Andrew, *J.M. Barrie and The Lost Boys*, (Yale University Press, Connecticut, 2003), p. 12
3. Barrie, J.M., *The Wedding Guest*, Collected Works of James M. Barrie, (Classic Books, Middlesex, 2001)
4. Birkin, Andrew, *J.M. Barrie and The Lost Boys*, (Yale University Press, Connecticut, 2003), p. 12

5. Barrie, J.M., *Margaret Ogilvy*, (Lightening Source UK Ltd., Milton Keynes, 2022), pp. 17-21
6. Barrie, J.M., *A Window in Thrums*, (The Saltire Society, Edinburgh, 2005), p. 29

Chapter 3

1. Kipling, Rudyard, *The Jungle Book*, (Macmillan, London, 1894)
2. Wells, H.G., *The War of the Worlds*, (William Heinemann, London, 1898)
3. Barrie, J.M., *Margaret Ogilvy*, (Lightening Source UK Ltd., Milton Keynes, 2022), pp. 43-44
4. Birkin, Andrew, *J.M. Barrie and The Lost Boys*, (Yale University Press, Connecticut, 2003), p. 22
5. Barrie, J.M. *Peter Pan*, (Suzeteo Enterprises, Greenwood, 2019), p. 25
6. Barrie, J.M. *Peter Pan*, (Suzeteo Enterprises, Greenwood, 2019), p. 98
7. Birkin, Andrew, *J.M. Barrie and The Lost Boys*, (Yale University Press, Connecticut, 2003), pp. 23-24
8. Barrie, J.M., *A Window in Thrums*, (The Saltire Society, Edinburgh, 2005), p. 90
9. Birkin, Andrew, *J.M. Barrie and The Lost Boys*, (Yale University Press, Connecticut, 2003)
10. Birkin, Andrew, *J.M. Barrie and The Lost Boys*, (Yale University Press, Connecticut, 2003), p. 30
11. Ansell, Mary, *Dogs and Men*, (Duckworth & Co., London, 1924)
12. Barrie, J.M., *Sentimental Tommy*, (Cassell & Company, London, 1896)
13. Barrie, J.M., *Margaret Ogilvy*, (Lightening Source UK Ltd., Milton Keynes, 2022), p. 61
14. Barrie, J.M., *Margaret Ogilvy*, (Lightening Source UK Ltd., Milton Keynes, 2022), p. 62
15. Barrie, J.M., *Margaret Ogilvy*, (Lightening Source UK Ltd., Milton Keynes, 2022), p. 62
16. Barrie, J.M., *Margaret Ogilvy*, (Lightening Source UK Ltd., Milton Keynes, 2022), p. 63
17. Barrie, J.M., *Margaret Ogilvy*, (Lightening Source UK Ltd., Milton Keynes, 2022), p. 64
18. Barrie, J.M., *The Little Minister*, (American Publishers Corporation, New York, 1897)

19. Barrie, J.M., *Tommy and Grizel*, (Createspace, North Charleston, 2004)
20. Barrie, J.M., *Tommy and Grizel*, (Createspace, North Charleston, 2004), p. 87
21. Barrie, J.M., *Tommy and Grizel*, (Createspace, North Charleston, 2004), p.197

Chapter 4

1. Maude, Pamela, *Worlds Away*, (John Baker, London, 1964), p. 137
2. Barrie, J.M., *Tommy and Grizel*, (Createspace, North Charleston, 2004)
3. Du Maurier, George, *Peter Ibbetson*, (McIlvaine & Co., 1891)
4. Du Maurier, George, *Trilby*, (Harper's Magazine, New York, 1895)
5. Du Maurier, Daphne, *Rebecca*, (Victor Gollancz Ltd., London, 1938)
6. Du Maurier, *Jamaica Inn*, (Victor Gollancz Ltd., London, 1936)
7. Birkin, Andrew, *J.M. Barrie and The Lost Boys*, (Yale University Press, Connecticut, 2003), p.66
8. Barrie, J.M., *The Little White Bird*, (Hodder & Stoughton, London, 1902)
9. See *Sources*: Collections, 1
10. Barrie, J.M., *The Little White Bird*, (Charles Scribners, New York, 1902), pp. 9-10
11. Barrie, J.M., *The Little White Bird*, (Charles Scribners, New York, 1902), p. 77
12. Barrie, J.M., *The Little White Bird*, (Charles Scribners, New York, 1902), p. 30
13. Barrie, J.M., *The Little White Bird*, (Charles Scribners, New York, 1902), p. 166
14. Barrie, J.M., *The Little White Bird*, (Charles Scribners, New York, 1902), pp. 207-208
15. Barrie, J.M. *Peter Pan*, (Suzeteo Enterprises, Greenwood, 2019), p. 6
16. Barrie, J.M. *Peter Pan*, (Suzeteo Enterprises, Greenwood, 2019), p. 88

Chapter 5

1. Barrie, J.M., *The Little White Bird*, (Charles Scribners, New York, 1902), pp. 313-314
2. See *Sources*: Collections, 1

3. Barrie, J.M., *The Boy Castaways of Black Lake Island*, (T. and A. Constable, Edinburgh, 1901), p. viii
4. See *Sources*: Collections, 2
5. Ansell, Mary, *Dogs and Men*, (Duckworth & Co., London, 1924), p. 42
6. See *Sources*: Collections, 4
7. Barrie, J.M., *The Little White Bird*, (Charles Scribners, New York, 1902), pp. 255-256
8. Barrie, J.M., *The Little White Bird*, (Charles Scribners, New York, 1902), pp. 258-259
9. Barrie, J.M., *The Little White Bird*, (Charles Scribners, New York, 1902), p. 259
10. Barrie, J.M., *The Little White Bird*, (Charles Scribners, New York, 1902), p. 56
11. See Sources, (number on the list) - Morgue
12. Ansell, Mary, *Dogs and Men*, (Duckworth & Co., London, 1924)
13. See Sources: Collections, 1
14. Barrie, J.M., *Peter Pan, or The Boy Who Wouldn't Grow Up*, (1904)
    Barrie, J.M., *Peter Pan, or The Boy Who Wouldn't Grow Up*, (Oxford University Press Inc., New York, 2008)
15. Du Maurier, Daphne, *Gerald: A Portrait*, (Gollancz, London, 1934)
16. See *Sources*: Collections, 1

Chapter 6

1. Barrie, J.M., *Peter Pan, or The Boy Who Wouldn't Grow Up*, (Oxford University Press Inc., New York, 2008), p. 137
2. Barrie, J.M., *Peter Pan, or The Boy Who Wouldn't Grow Up*, (Oxford University Press Inc., New York, 2008), p. 128
3. Barrie, J.M., *Peter Pan, or The Boy Who Wouldn't Grow Up*, (Oxford University Press Inc., New York, 2008), p. 151
4. See *Sources*: Collections, 1
5. Barrie, J.M. *Peter Pan*, (Suzeteo Enterprises, Greenwood, 2019), p. 152
6. Barrie, J.M., *A Window in Thrums*, (The Saltire Society, Edinburgh, 2005), p. 29
7. Barrie, J.M., *Peter Pan, or The Boy Who Wouldn't Grow Up*, (Oxford University Press Inc., New York, 2008), p. 108

Notes

8. Barrie, J.M., *Peter Pan, or The Boy Who Wouldn't Grow Up*, (Oxford University Press Inc., New York, 2008), pp. 129-130
9. Barrie, J.M., *Peter Pan, or The Boy Who Wouldn't Grow Up*, (Oxford University Press Inc., New York, 2008), p. 89
10. Barrie, J.M., *Peter Pan, or The Boy Who Wouldn't Grow Up*, (Oxford University Press Inc., New York, 2008), pp. 107-112
11. Birkin, Andrew, *J.M. Barrie and The Lost Boys*, (Yale University Press, Connecticut, 2003), p. 124
12. Birkin, Andrew, *J.M. Barrie and The Lost Boys*, (Yale University Press, Connecticut, 2003), p. 130
13. Barrie, J.M., *Peter Pan, or The Boy Who Wouldn't Grow Up*, (Oxford University Press Inc., New York, 2008), p. 112
14. Barrie, J.M., *Peter Pan, or The Boy Who Wouldn't Grow Up*, (Oxford University Press Inc., New York, 2008), p. 102
15. Barrie, J.M., *Peter Pan, or The Boy Who Wouldn't Grow Up*, (Oxford University Press Inc., New York, 2008), p. 125
16. Barrie, J.M., *Peter Pan, or The Boy Who Wouldn't Grow Up*, (Oxford University Press Inc., New York, 2008), p. 159
17. Barrie, J.M., *Peter Pan, or The Boy Who Wouldn't Grow Up*, (Oxford University Press Inc., New York, 2008), p. 153
18. Barrie, J.M., *Peter Pan, or The Boy Who Wouldn't Grow Up*, (Oxford University Press Inc., New York, 2008), p. 151
19. See *Sources*: Collections, 1
20. Barrie, J.M., *Peter Pan, or The Boy Who Wouldn't Grow Up*, (Oxford University Press Inc., New York, 2008), p. 135

Chapter 7

1. See *Sources*: Collections, 4
2. Letter from Dolly Ponsonby to Peter Llewelyn Davies, December 1946
3. See *Sources*: Collections, 2
4. See *Sources*: Collections, 2
5. See *Sources*: Collections, 2
6. Letter from Arthur Llewelyn Davies to his father, John Llewelyn Davies, 4th June 1906
7. Birkin, Andrew, *J.M. Barrie and The Lost Boys*, (Yale University Press, Connecticut, 2003), p. 135

8. Birkin, Andrew, *J.M. Barrie and The Lost Boys*, (Yale University Press, Connecticut, 2003), p. 137
9. See *Sources*: Collections, 2
10. Letter from Sylvia Llewelyn Davies to Margaret Llewelyn Davies, July 1906
11. See *Sources*: Collections, 2
12. Letter from Arthur Llewelyn Davies to Margaret Llewelyn Davies, August 6th 1906
13. See *Sources*: Collections, 4
14. See *Sources*: Collections, 2
15. See *Sources*: Collections, 2
16. Birkin, Andrew, *J.M. Barrie and The Lost Boys*, (Yale University Press, Connecticut, 2003), p. 145
17. See *Sources*: Collections, 2
18. Barrie, J.M., *Peter Pan in Kensington Gardens*, (Hodder and Stoughton, London, 1906)
19. See *Sources*: Collections, 2
20. See *Sources*: Collections, 2
21. See *Sources*: Collections, 2
22. See *Sources*: Collections, 1
23. See *Sources*: Collections, 2
24. See *Sources*: Collections, 2

Chapter 8

1. Letter from Sylvia Llewelyn Davies to Dolly Ponsonby, May 1907
2. See *Sources*: Collections, 2
3. See *Sources*: Collections, 2
4. See *Sources*: Collections, 2
5. See *Sources*: Collections, 2
6. See *Sources*: Collections, 2
7. Barrie, J.M. *Peter Pan*, (Suzeteo Enterprises, Greenwood, 2019), p. 118
8. See *Sources*: Collections, 2
9. See *Sources*: Collections, 2
10. See *Sources*: Websites, 32
11. See *Sources*: Websites, 32
12. Letter from Nico Llewelyn Davies to Andrew Birkin, 1976

13. See *Sources*: Websites, 32
14. See *Sources*: Collections, 2
15. Blow, Sydney, *Through the Stage Doors*, (Chambers, London, 1958)
16. Barrie, J.M. *Peter Pan*, (Suzeteo Enterprises, Greenwood, 2019), pp. 161-165
17. Mackail, Denis, *The Story of J.M.B.*, (Peter Davies Ltd., London, 1941)
18. See *Sources*: Collections, 2
19. See *Sources*: Collections, 4
20. Birkin, Andrew, *J.M. Barrie and The Lost Boys*, (Yale University Press, Connecticut, 2003), p. 170
21. Taped interview with Geraldine Llewelyn Davies, March 1976, See *Sources*: Websites, 32
22. See *Sources*: Collections, 2
23. See *Sources*: Collections, 2
24. Court transcript as published in *The Daily Telegraph* and *Daily Mail*, 14th October 1909
25. Birkin, Andrew, *J.M. Barrie and The Lost Boys*, (Yale University Press, Connecticut, 2003), p. 177
26. Birkin, Andrew, *J.M. Barrie and The Lost Boys*, (Yale University Press, Connecticut, 2003), p. 176
27. See *Sources*: Collections, 1
28. Court transcript as published in *The Daily Telegraph* and *Daily Mail*, 14th October 1909
29. Letter from Mary Ansell to H.G. Wells, 21st October 1909

Chapter 9

1. See *Sources*: Collections, 2
2. See *Sources*: Collections, 2
3. Letter from Beatrix du Maurier to Marie du Maurier, 17th October 1909
4. See *Sources*: Collections, 2
5. Taped interview with Mrs Norma Douglas Henry, March 1978, See *Sources*: Websites, 32
6. See *Sources*: Collections, 2
7. See *Sources*: Collections, 2
8. Letter from Dolly Ponsonby to Peter Davies, December 1946

9. Letter from Emma du Maurier to Marie du Maurier, 1st August 1910
10. Letter from Emma du Maurier to Marie du Maurier, 1st August 1910
11. Letter from Emma du Maurier to Marie du Maurier, 1st August 1910
12. See *Sources*: Collections, 2
13. See *Sources*: Collections, 2
14. See *Sources*: Collections, 2
15. See *Sources*: Collections, 2
16. Mackail, Denis, *The Story of J.M.B.*, (Peter Davies Ltd., London, 1941), p. 426
17. Letter from Emma du Maurier to Marie du Maurier, 27th August 1910
18. See *Sources*: Collections, 2
19. Letter from Jack Llewelyn Davies to Peter Davies, 1952
20. See *Sources*: Collections, 2

Chapter 10

1. See *Sources*: Collections, 2
2. See *Sources*: Websites, 32
3. See *Sources*: Collections, 2
4. See *Sources*: Collections, 2
5. See *Sources*: Collections, 2
6. Letter from J.M. Barrie to Arthur Quiller-Couch, 7th March 1911
7. Barrie, J.M. *Peter Pan*, (Suzeteo Enterprises, Greenwood, 2019), p. 158
8. See *Sources*: Collections, 1
9. Letter from J.M. Barrie to Nurse Loosemore, 17th September 1911
10. See *Sources*: Collections, 4
11. See *Sources*: Websites, 32
12. See *Sources*: Collections, 1
13. Birkin, Andrew, *J.M. Barrie and The Lost Boys*, (Yale University Press, Connecticut, 2003), p. 206
14. See *Sources*: Collections, 2

Chapter 11

1. Letter from J.M. Barrie to Charles Turley-Smith, April 1913
2. Barrie, J.M., *Dear Brutus*, (Hodder and Stoughton, London, 1935)

Notes

3. Barrie, J.M., *A Window in Thrums*, (The Saltire Society, Edinburgh, 2005), p. 116
4. See *Sources*: Collections, 2
5. Barrie, J.M., *Peter Pan*, (Suzeteo Enterprises, Greenwood, 2019), p. 165
6. Chase, Pauline, *Peter Pan's Postbag*, (William Heinemann, London, 1909)
7. See *Sources*: Collections, 2
8. Letter from J.M. Barrie to Lord Auberon Thomas Herbert, 9th Baron Lucas and 5th Lord Dingwall, 4th August 1914
9. See *Sources*: Collections, 2
10. See *Sources*: Collections, 2
11. See *Sources*: Collections, 2
12. See *Sources*: Websites, 32
13. Barrie, J.M. *Peter Pan*, (Suzeteo Enterprises, Greenwood, 2019), p. 30

Chapter 12

1. See *Sources*: Collections, 1
2. See *Sources*: Collections, 2
3. See *Sources*: Collections, 2
4. See *Sources*: Collections, 1
5. See *Sources*: Collections, 2
6. See *Sources*: Collections, 1
7. See *Sources*: Collections, 2
8. See *Sources*: Collections, 1
9. Letter from Guy du Maurier to his wife, Gwendolyn Maye Price
10. See *Sources*: Collections, 2
11. See *Sources*: Collections, 2
12. See *Sources*: Collections, 1
13. See *Sources*: Collections, 2
14. Letter from Aubrey Tennyson to Peter Davies, March 1915

Chapter 13

1. See *Sources*: Collections, 2
2. Birkin, Andrew, *J.M. Barrie and The Lost Boys*, (Yale University Press, Connecticut, 2003), p. 243

3. See *Sources*: Collections, 2
4. See *Sources*: Collections, 1
5. See *Sources*: Collections, 2
6. Nash, Percy, *Rosy Rapture*, (Neptune Film Co., 1915)
7. Marcosson, Isaac F.; Frohman, David, *Charles Frohman : Manager and Man*, (The Bodley Head, London, 1916), p. 386
8. See *Sources*: Websites, 32
9. See *Sources*: Collections, 5
10. See *Sources*: Collections, 5

Chapter 14

1. See *Sources*: Websites, 32
2. See *Sources*: Websites, 32
3. See *Sources*: Websites, 32
4. See *Sources*: Websites, 32
5. See *Sources*: Websites, 32

Chapter 15

1. See *Sources*: Collections, 1
2. Lucas, E.V., (The Times, 21st May 1921)
3. Birkin, Andrew, *J.M. Barrie and The Lost Boys*, (Yale University Press, Connecticut, 2003), p. 282
4. See *Sources*: Websites, 32
5. See *Sources*: Websites, 32
6. Birkin, Andrew, *J.M. Barrie and The Lost Boys*, (Yale University Press, Connecticut, 2003), p. 283
7. Letter from Nico Llewelyn Davies to Andrew Birkin, 1975
8. See *Sources*: Websites, 32
9. See *Sources*: Websites, 32
10. Mackail, Denis, *The Story of J.M.B.*, (Peter Davies Ltd., London, 1941)
11. Barrie, J.M., *Shall We Join the Ladies?*, (Hodder and Stoughton, London, 1929)
12. See *Sources*: Collections, 1

13. *Oxford Times* article, 27th May 1921
14. Letter from Nico Llewelyn Davies to Andrew Birkin, December 1975
15. *The Evening Standard*, 21st May 1921

Chapter 16

1. Letter from Nico Llewelyn Davies to Andrew Birkin, December 1975
2. Asquith, Cynthia, *Lady Cynthia Asquith Diaries: 1915-1918*, (Hutchinson, London, 1968)
3. Letter from J.M. Barrie to Lady Elizabeth Lucas, December 1921
4. Letter from J.M. Barrie to Robin Dundas, December 1921
5. See *Sources*: Collections, 1
6. Birkin, Andrew, *J.M. Barrie and The Lost Boys*, (Yale University Press, Connecticut, 2003), p. 298
7. Letter from J.M. Barrie to Robin Dundas, November 1922
8. Birkin, Andrew, *J.M. Barrie and The Lost Boys*, (Yale University Press, Connecticut, 2003), p. 295
9. See *Sources*: Collections, 1
10. Brenon, Herbert, *Peter Pan*, (Paramount Pictures, 1924)
11. Duguid, Laura, *The Legacy of Pan - on the set of Peter Pan (2003)*, interviewed by Sarah Ferguson https://www.youtube.com/watch?v=1_cf5Ks9SUo Time: 4:45
12. Birkin, Andrew, *J.M. Barrie and The Lost Boys*, (Yale University Press, Connecticut, 2003), p. 299
13. Barrie, J.M., *The Boy David*, (Charles Scribner's Sons, New York, 1938)

Chapter 17

1. Interview with Ruthven Llewelyn Davies for the *Sunday Times*, January 1995
2. See *Sources*: Collections, 2
3. See *Sources*: Websites, 32
4. Letter from Jack Llewelyn Davies, 1952
5. Bennett, Rodney, *The Lost Boys*, (BBC, 1978)

6. Duguid, Laura, *The Legacy of Pan - on the set of Peter Pan (2003)*, interviewed by Sarah Ferguson https://www.youtube.com/watch?v=1_cf5Ks9SUo Time: 4:02
7. Forster, Marc, *Finding Neverland*, (Mirimax, 2004)
8. Rennell, Tony, *The monster of Neverland: How JM Barrie did a 'Peter Pan' and stole another couple's children*, (Mail Online, 8th July 2008)
9. Grahame, Kenneth, *The Wind in the Willows*, (Methuen, London, 1908)
10. Milne, A.A., *Winnie-the-Pooh*, (Methuen, London, 1926)

Epilogue

1. McCaughrean, Geraldine, *Peter Pan in Scarlet*, (Oxford University Press, Oxford, 2006)
2. Hand, David, et al., *Snow White and the Seven Dwarfs*, (Walt Disney Productions, 1937)
3. Burnes, Brian; Viets, Dan; Butler, Robert W., *Walt Disney's Missouri: The Roots of a Creative Genius* (Kansas Cirt Star Books, Kansas, 2002), p. 31
4. Luske, Hamilton; Geronimi, Clyde; Jackson, Wilfred, *Peter Pan*, (Walt Disney Productions, 1953)
5. Crowther, Bosley, *The Screen in Review: Disney's 'Peter Pan' Bows*, (The New York Times, 12th February 1953), p. 23
6. Budd, Robin, *Peter Pan in: Return to Neverland*, (Walt Disney Pictures; Disney MovieToons; Walt Disney Television Animation, 2002)
7. Dietz, Damion, *Neverland*, (New Media Entertainment, 2003)
8. Waterfield, Rhys, *Peter Pan's Neverland Nightmare*, (ITN Studios; Jagged Edge Productions, 2024)
9. Zeitlin, Benh, *Wendy*, (Searchlight Pictures, 2020)
10. Spielberg, Steven, *Hook*, (TriStar Pictures, 1991), 02h 15m 01s
11. Hogan, P.J., *Peter Pan*, (Universal Pictures, 2003), 01h 40m 50s
12. Tatar, Maria, *The Annotated Peter Pan: The Centennial Edition*, (Norton and Co., New York, 2011), p. 334
13. Lowery, David, *Peter Pan and Wendy*, (Disney+, 2023)
14. Lowery, David, *Peter Pan and Wendy*, (Disney+, 2023), 01h 29m 24s